F...
Provence &
the Riviera

Reprinted from *Fodor's France*

Fodor's Travel Publications, Inc.
New York • Toronto • London • Sydney • Auckland

Fodor's Provence & the Riviera

Editor: Nancy van Itallie
Editorial Contributors: Nancy Coons, Simon Hewitt, Jillian Magalaner, Marcy Pritchard, Melanie Roth
Creative Director: Fabrizio La Rocca
Cartographer: David Lindroth
Illustrator: Karl Tanner
Cover Photograph: Pascal Perret/Image Bank

Design: Vignelli Associates

Special Sales

Fodor's Travel Publications are available at special discounts for bulk purchases (100 copies or more) for sales promotions or premiums. Special editions, including personalized covers, excerpts of existing guides, and corporate imprints, can be created in large quantities for special needs. For more information, write to Special Marketing, Fodor's Travel Publications, 201 E. 50th Street, New York, NY 10022. Inquiries from Canada should be sent to Random House of Canada, Ltd., Marketing Department, 1265 Aerowood Drive, Mississauga, Ontario L4W 1B9. Inquiries from the United Kingdom should be sent to Fodor's Travel Publications, 20 Vauxhall Bridge Road, London, England SW1V 2SA.

Contents

Maps

Foreword

Special thanks to Marion Fourestier of the French Tourist Office in New York; and to Brigitte Doignon and Florence Danjean.

While every care has been taken to ensure the accuracy of the information in this guide, the passage of time will always bring change and, consequently, the publisher cannot accept responsibility for errors that may occur.

All prices and opening times quoted here are based on information supplied to us at press time. Hours and admission fees may change, however, and the prudent traveler will avoid inconvenience by calling ahead.

Fodor's wants to hear about your travel experiences, both pleasant and unpleasant. When a hotel or restaurant fails to live up to its billing, let us know and we will investigate the complaint and revise our entries where the facts warrant it.

Send your letters to the editors of Fodor's Travel Publications, 201 East 50th Street, New York, NY 10022.

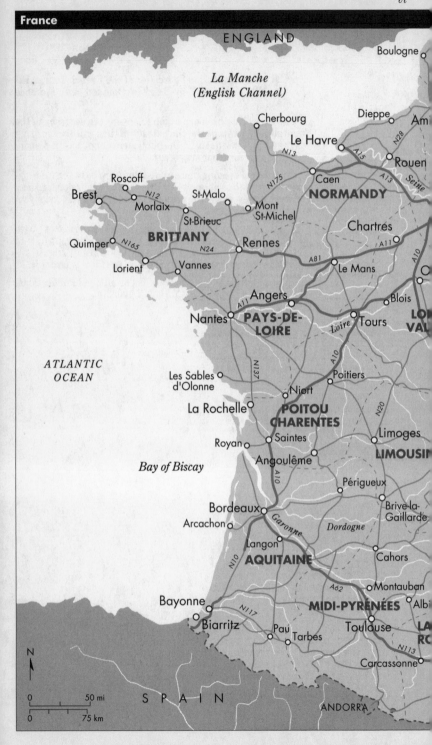

France

ENGLAND

La Manche
(English Channel)

Boulogne

Cherbourg

Dieppe

Ami

N28

Le Havre

N13

A15

Rouen

A13

Seine

Caen

NORMANDY

N175

Roscoff

N12

St-Malo

Brest

Morlaix

St-Brieuc

Mont
St-Michel

Chartres

A11

BRITTANY

N24

Rennes

A10

Quimper

N165

Vannes

A81

Le Mans

LO
VAL

Lorient

Angers

A11

Blois

Nantes

PAYS-DE-
LOIRE

Loire

Tours

ATLANTIC
OCEAN

Les Sables
d'Olonne

N137

Poitiers

A10

La Rochelle

Niort

POITOU
CHARENTES

N20

Royan

Saintes

Limoges

LIMOUSIN

Bay of Biscay

Angoulême

A10

Périgueux

Brive-la-
Gaillarde

Bordeaux

Garonne

Arcachon

Dordogne

Langon

N10

AQUITAINE

Cahors

A62

Montauban

Bayonne

N117

MIDI-PYRÉNÉES

Albi

Biarritz

Pau

Tarbes

Toulouse

LA
RO

N113

Carcassonne

N

0   50 mi

0   75 km

S P A I N

ANDORRA

Introduction

By Nancy Coons

Author of Fodor's Switzerland '92 *and a contributor to* Fodor's Europe, *Nancy Coons has written on European topics for* The Wall Street Journal, Opera News, *and* European Travel and Life. *She lives in Luxembourg with her husband Mark Olsen, who plays horn in the Orchestra de Radio-Tele-Luxembourg and their daughter Elodie.*

Sun-bleached, the roasted red clay roofs of the stone cottages skew downhill at Cubist angles, each Romanesque tile, in its snaking row, as alike and as varied as the reeds in a Pan pipe; together, their broad horizontal flow forms a foil for the dark, thrusting verticals of the funeral cypress, the ephemeral, feminine puff of the silvery olive. In the fields behind, white-hot at midday, chill and spare at night, you can stoop down along the pathside and pick wild thyme, rosemary, lavender dried in the arid breeze; their acrid-sweet scent cuts through the crystal air like smelling salts. Goat- and sheep-bells tinkle behind rock walls, and churchbells sound across valleys as easily as over the village wall. Nowhere in France, perhaps nowhere in the Western World, can you touch antiquity with this intimacy—its exoticism, its purity, eternal and alive. Provence and the Côte d'Azur: *Le sud de France* is, as the French say, *primordial.*

Basking luxuriously along the sunny southern flank of France, bordered to the east by Italy, sheltered to the northeast by the Alps, and leaning west and southwest toward its Spanish-influenced neighbors in Languedoc and the Basque country, Provence and its nearby coast, the Riviera, are to the Mediterranean as Eve was to Adam's rib, begotten, as it were, by the Fertile Crescent. The Greeks and Phoenicians first brought classical culture to the Celtic natives of Gaul in 600 BC when they founded Massilia (Marseille), which thrived as a colony until the Ligurians began to impose on them. By the 2nd century BC, Romans were called in for military reinforcement, and turned their weapons on the Greeks instead.

Thus came to be *Provincia Romana*, the first Roman stronghold in Gaul, where the best of Latin culture flourished until the fall of the Empire. Under Roman rule, the Gauls were transformed (as one period writer had it) from "mustachioed, abundantly hairy, exuberant, audacious, thoughtless, boastful, passionate warriors" into disciplined hard workers—at least temporarily. In its wake, Rome left its physical mark as well: The theater and triumphal arch at Orange; more arches at Cavaillon and Carpentras; the amphitheater at Nîmes, the aqueduct at Pont-du-Gard; the mausoleum at St-Remy-de-Provence; the temple of Augustus and Livia (of *I, Claudius* fame) at Vienne—these monuments, still standing today, are considered among the best of their kind in existence, easily rivaling the Colosseum in Rome; the Maison carrée at Nîmes, built by Agrippa in 16 BC, remains as pure an homage to their Greek forebears as the Romans ever produced. Vivid details in Roman artifacts bring the stories to life: The creamy marble bust of Octavian found at Arles shows a peach-fuzz beard on his all-too-young face—a Roman sign of mourning for the assassination of Julius Caesar.

Yet the noble remains of Rome have taken on a patina and given way to the culture of modern Provence, where the hustling, burly streetlife of Marseille still punches out at *sieste* time for a milky *pastis* (the local, anise-based aperitif), a bowl of nutty black olives, or a game of *boules*. Today, the south of France implies a lazy, laissez-faire lifestyle, a barefoot idyll, three-hour lunches, sultry terrace nights, and a splash in the Mediterranean. In fact, most of the hordes of both French and foreign tourists that descend on Provence and the Riviera today think Caesar is a salad, though they might be able to name the last five film directors to place at Cannes. Far from searching for the classical perfection of a 2nd-century column, they seek out the glamor that drew Grace Kelly and other Hollywood stars of the '50s—who were in turn drawn by the gentry and the international literary jet-set, the Nicks and Noras of the Lost Generation. On these slim rocky beaches, if anywhere in the world, were nurtured the first Perfect Tans, cultivated with tantalizing exhibitionism on every flauntable inch of skin. And still today, oblivious to the Ozone Hole, rank on rank of nearly bare bodies crowd flank to flank on the Mediterranean shore.

Yet caveat emptor—the glamour of the Riviera has, for the most part, been crowded down to the shoreline and swept out to sea: honky-tonk tourist traps and project-like high rises dominate much of the region, while the wealthy hoard their seaside serenity in private, isolated villas. At greasy brasseries along the waterfront, sunburned visitors and leathery locals fight for the waiter's attention just to gulp down a *'ot dog* and a lukewarm Coke, or to strain through the canned crab in a mass-produced *bourride*.

To find the grace and antiquity of the region, and the sun if not the beach, visitors would do well to hunt out the smaller towns, both nestled along the waterfront and rising like ziggurats on stony hilltops behind the coast. Here, you'll discover the crystalline light and elemental forms that inspired Cezanne, Pissarro, Bonnard, Van Gogh, Matisse, Braque, Léger, Miró, Chagall, and Picasso. The *volupté* of the Mediterranean saturates their work—sensual fruit, lush flowers, fundamental forms, light and color analyzed, interpreted, transformed, revealed. They, like the literati who retreat here today, found in this primeval setting the peace and stimulation to create.

That's the sort of epiphany you may face in *le Sud*, whether standing humbled inside the 5th-century baptistry in Saint-Sauveur at Aix; breakfasting on a wrought-iron balcony overlooking turquoise Mediterranean tides; contemplating the orbs and linear perspective of a melon field outside Cavaillon; or sipping the sea-perfumed elixir of a great bouillabaisse (surely the Phoenicians sipped something similar 2,600 years ago) along the piers of Marseille. Provocative, tranquil, earthy, primordial: Like a woven rope of garlic, it's the essence of Latin France.

1 Essential Information

Before You Go

Government Tourist Offices

Contact the French Government Tourist Offices for information on all aspects of travel to and in Provence and the Riviera.

In the U.S. 610 Fifth Ave., New York, NY 10020 (tel. 212/315–0888); 645 N. Michigan Ave., Chicago, IL 60611 (tel. 312/337–6301); 2305 Cedar Springs Rd., Dallas, TX 75201 (tel. 214/720–4010); 9454 Wilshire Blvd., Suite 303, Beverly Hills, CA 90212 (tel. 213/271–6665); 1 Hallidie Plaza, Suite 250, San Francisco, CA 94102 (tel. 415/986–4174).

In Canada 1981 McGill College, Suite 490, Montreal, Quebec H3A 2W9 (tel. 514/288–4264); 1 Dundas St. W., Suite 2405, Box 8, Toronto, Ontario M5G 1Z3 (tel. 416/593–4723).

In the U.K. 178 Piccadilly, London W1V OAL England (tel. 071/491–7622).

Tour Groups

Care to sip wine in the vineyard of Provence or discover the sources of the Impressionist inspiration? Then you may want to consider a package tour. Creative itineraries abound, offering access to places you may not be able to get to on your own as well as the more traditional spots. They also tend to save you money on airfare and hotels. If group outings are not your style, check into independent packages; somewhat more expensive than package tours, they are also more flexible.

When considering a tour, be sure to find out exactly what expenses are included (particularly tips, taxes, side trips, additional meals, and entertainment); governmental ratings of all hotels on the itinerary and the facilities they offer; cancellation policies for both you and the tour operator; and, if you are traveling alone, the price of the single supplement. Most tour operators request that bookings be made through a travel agent (there is no additional charge for doing so). Below is a sampling of the many tour options that are available. Contact your travel agent or the French Government Tourist Office for additional resources.

General-Interest Tours **Jet Vacations** (1775 Broadway, Suite 2405, New York, NY 10019, tel. 212/247–0999 or 800/538–0999) offers a 7-day "Monte Carlo Magnifique" package. **Maupintour** (Box 807, Lawrence, KA 66044, tel. 800/255–4266 or 913/843–1211) offers 14-day packages to both areas.

In the United Kingdom, **Thomas Cook** (36 Thorpe Wood, Peterborough PE3 6SB, tel. 0733/332255) offers either escorted tours or packages for the independent traveler.

Special-Interest Tours *Wine/Cuisine* **Travel Concepts** (373 Commonwealth Ave., Suite 601, Boston, MA 02115–1815, tel. 617/266–8450) offers tours of Provence and the Riviera that combine wine, cuisine, history, and art, or can plan itineraries that feature one of these interests.

Art/Architecture In the United Kingdom, **Prospect Music & Art Tours Ltd.** (454-458 Chiswick High Rd., London W4 5TT, tel. 081/995–2151) offers "Roman Provence" and "Art in the South of France," 7-day art and architecture tours hosted by a guest lecturer.

Music   **Dailey-Thorp Travel** (315 W. 57th St., New York, NY 10019, tel. 212/307–1555) offers music tours, including one to the annual Aix-en-Provence Festival of Lyric Art and Music. Itineraries vary according to available performances.

In the United Kingdom, **Prospect Music & Art Tours Ltd.** (*see* Art/Architecture, *above*) also offers a trip to the Aix-en-Provence music festival.

Package Deals for Independent Travelers

Self-drive tours are popular in France, and **The French Experience** (370 Lexington Ave., Suite 812, New York, NY 10017, tel. 212/986–1115 or 212/986–3800) has put together different routes, including "Adventuring in Provence," which includes horseback riding, bicycling, and a photography trip. Accommodations at country cottages can also be arranged or try their "French à la Carte" menu of hotel packages in Nice. **Abercrombie & Kent International** (1420 Kensington Rd., Oak Brook, IL 60521, tel. 708/954–2944 or 800/323–7308) adds the option of a chauffeur to its somewhat pricier deluxe driving tours. **Air France** (120 W. 56th St., New York, NY 10017, tel. 212/247–0100) offers week-long air/hotel packages to the Riviera. "France à la Carte" is a menu of hotel packages available in Nice from **The French Experience** (*see above*). **American Airlines Fly AAway Vacations** (tel. 817/355–1234 or 800/433–7300) lets you design your own fly/drive itinerary from a selection of hotels, rental cars, and rail passes.

In the United Kingdom, **Thomas Cook** (*see* General-Interest Tours, *above*) offers packages for the independent traveler with a representative on site to help out if needed.

When to Go

On the whole, June and September are the best months to be in Provence, as both are free of the midsummer crowds. June offers the advantage of long daylight hours, while slightly lower prices and frequent Indian summers (often lasting well into October) make September an attractive proposition.

Try to avoid the second half of July and all of August, or be prepared for inflated prices and huge crowds on the roads and beaches. Don't travel on or around July 14 and August 1, 14, and 31. July and August in southern France can be stifling.

Anytime between March and November will offer you a good chance to soak up the sun on the Riviera, though, of course, you'll tan quicker between June and September.

Climate   The following are average daily maximum and minimum temperatures for Nice.

Nice	Jan.	55F	13C	**May**	68F	20C	**Sept.**	77F	25C
		39	4		55	13		61	16
	Feb.	55F	13C	**June**	75F	24C	**Oct.**	70F	21C
		41	5		61	16		54	12
	Mar.	59F	15C	**July**	81F	27C	**Nov.**	63F	17C
		45	7		64	18		46	8
	Apr.	64F	18C	**Aug.**	81F	27C	**Dec.**	55F	13C
		46	8		64	18		41	5

Current weather information for foreign and domestic cities may be obtained by calling the **Weather Channel Connection** at 900/932–8437 from a touch-tone phone. In addition to offering the weather report, the Weather Channel Connection offers local time and travel tips, as well as hurricane, foliage, and ski reports. The call costs 95¢ per minute.

Public Holidays   January 1, Easter Monday, May 1 (Labor Day), May 8 (VE Day), Ascension Day (five weeks after Easter), the Monday after Pentecost, July 14 (Bastille Day), August 15 (Assumption), November 1 (All Saints), November 11 (Armistice), and Christmas Day. If a public holiday falls on a Tuesday or a Thursday, many businesses and shops and some restaurants close on the Monday or Friday, too.

Festivals and Seasonal Events

Top seasonal events in Provence and the Riviera include the Monte Carlo Motor Rally in January, February's Carnival in Nice, and the Cannes Film Festival in May. Contact the French Government Tourist Office for exact dates and further information.

Jan. International Circus Festival, featuring top acts from around the world, is held in Monaco.

Mid- to late Jan. Monte Carlo Motor Rally, one of the motoring world's most venerable races, has its finish line in the streets of Monaco.

Mid- to late Feb. Carnival of Nice provides an exotic blend of parades and revelry during the weeks leading up to Lent.

Mid- to late Apr. Monte Carlo Open Tennis Championships get under way at the ultraswank Monte Carlo Country Club.

Mid- to late May. Cannes Film Festival sees two weeks of star-studded events.

Mid-May. Monaco Grand Prix races through the streets of Monaco.

Early July to early Aug. Festival of Avignon affords almost an entire month of top-notch theater throughout Avignon. (Tickets: Bureau de Festival, 8-bis rue de Mons, 84000 Avignon, tel. 90–82–67–08.)

Mid-July. Grand Parade of Jazz provides nearly two weeks of musical entertainment in Nice.

July 14. Bastille Day, a national holiday commemorated throughout the country, celebrates the storming of the Bastille in Paris in 1789—the start of the French Revolution.

Mid- to late July. Festival of Lyric Art and Music brings nearly three weeks of musical entertainment to Aix-en-Provence. (Tickets: 32 pl. des Martyrs, 13100 Aix-en-Provence, tel. 42–21–14–40.)

Mid-July to early Aug. International Fireworks Festival features spectacular displays of pyrotechnics in Monaco.

Oct. *Vendanges* (grape harvest) festivals are held in the country's wine regions.

Dec. 24. Shepherd's Festival, a Christmas celebration, featuring midnight mass and picturesque "living crèches," is held in Les Baux, Provence.

What to Pack

Pack light: Baggage carts are scarce in airports and railroad stations, and luggage restrictions on international flights are tight. (*See* Carry-on Luggage and Checked Luggage, *below*, for exact specifications.)

Clothing What you pack depends more on the time of year than on any particular dress code. Eastern France is hot in the summer and cold in the winter. You'll need a sweater or warm jacket for the Mediterranean areas during the winter.

For the cities, pack as you would for an American city: cocktail outfits for formal restaurants and nightclubs, casual clothes for sightseeing. Jeans, as popular in France as anywhere else, are acceptable for sightseeing and informal dining. However, a jeans-and-sneakers outfit will cause raised eyebrows at theaters or expensive restaurants or when visiting French families. The rule here is to dress up rather than down. The exception is in young or bohemian circles, where casual dress is always acceptable.

Men and women who wear shorts will probably be denied admission to churches and cathedrals, although there is no longer any need for women to cover their heads and arms. For the beach resorts, pack something to wear over your bathing suit when you leave the beach (wearing bathing suits on the street is frowned upon).

Most casinos and nightclubs along the Riviera require jackets and ties. They are the place for chic cocktail dresses and tuxedos if you like to dress formally.

Miscellaneous You'll need an adapter for hair dryers and other small appliances. The electrical current in France is 220 volts and 50 cycles. If you are staying in budget hotels, take along small bars of soap; many either do not provide soap or limit guests to one tiny bar per room.

Carry-on Luggage Airlines generally allow each passenger one piece of carry-on luggage on international flights from the United States. The bag cannot exceed 45 inches—length + width + height—and must fit under the seat or in the overhead luggage compartment.

Checked Luggage Passengers are generally allowed to check two pieces of luggage, neither of which can exceed 62 inches—length + width + height—or weigh more than 70 pounds. Baggage allowances vary slightly among airlines, so be sure to check with the carrier or your travel agent before departure.

Taking Money Abroad

Traveler's checks and major U.S. credit cards—particularly Visa, often going under the name of France's domestic equivalent, Carte Bleue—are accepted in large towns and tourist areas. In small towns and rural areas, you'll need cash. Even in large cities, many small restaurants and shops operate on a cash basis. It's wise to change a small amount of money into

French francs before you go to avoid long lines at airport currency-exchange booths. Most U.S. banks will change your money into francs. If your local bank can't provide this service, you can exchange money through **Thomas Cook Currency Services.** To find the office nearest you, contact the headquarters (630 Fifth Ave., New York, NY 10111, tel. 212/757–6915).

The most widely recognized traveler's checks are **American Express, Barclay's, Thomas Cook,** and those issued through major commercial banks such as **Citibank** and **Bank of America.** (American Express now offers "AMEX Travelers Cheques for Two," which allow two people to sign and use the same checks.) Some banks will issue the checks free to established customers, but most charge a 1% commission fee. Buy part of the traveler's checks in small denominations to cash toward the end of your trip. This will save you from having to cash a large check and ending up with more francs than you need. (Hold on to your receipts after exchanging your traveler's checks; it's easier to convert foreign currency back into dollars if you have these receipts.) You can also buy traveler's checks in francs, a good idea if the dollar is falling and you want to lock in the current rate. Don't forget to take the addresses of offices where you can obtain refunds for lost or stolen traveler's checks. *The American Express Traveler's Companion,* a directory of offices to contact worldwide in case of loss or theft of American Express traveler's checks, is available at most travel-service locations.

Getting Money from Home

There are several ways to get money from home: (1) Have it sent through a large commercial bank with a branch in the town where you're staying. The only sticking point is that you must have an account with the bank; if you don't, you'll have to go through your bank, and the process will be slower and more expensive. (2) Have it sent through American Express. If you are a cardholder, you may cash a personal check or a counter check at an American Express office for up to $1,000; up to $500 will be in cash and $500 in traveler's checks. There is a 1% commission on the traveler's checks. American Express has a new service, **American Express MoneyGram,** available in France and most major cities worldwide. Through this service, even noncardholders can receive up to $10,000 in cash. It works this way: You call home and ask someone to go to an American Express office or an American Express MoneyGram agent located in a retail outlet and fill out an American Express MoneyGram (it can be paid for with cash or any major credit card). The person who makes the payment is given a reference number and telephones you with that number. The American Express MoneyGram agent calls an 800 number and authorizes the transfer of funds to an American Express office or a participating agency in the town where you're staying. In most cases, the money is available immediately on a 24-hour basis. You pick it up by showing identification and giving the reference number that was phoned to you by the person who purchased the American Express MoneyGram. Fees vary according to the amount of money sent. For sending $300, the fee is $30; for $5,000, $195. (For the American Express MoneyGram location nearest your home and for locations overseas, call 800/543–4080.) You do not have to be a cardholder to use this service. (3) Have it sent through **Western Union** (U.S. number: 800/325–6000). If you have a MasterCard or Visa, you can have money sent for any amount up to your credit limit. If not, have someone take cash or a certified cashier's check to a Western Union office. The money will be delivered to a bank in the city where you're staying within two business days. Fees vary with the amount of money sent. For sending $1,000, the fee is $64; for $500, $54.

French Currency

The units of currency in France are the franc (fr.) and the centime. Bills are in denominations of 500, 200, 100, 50, and 20 francs. Coins are 10, 5, 2, and 1 francs and 50, 20, 10, and 5 centimes. At press time (Fall '92), the exchange rate was about 5.05 francs to the U.S. dollar, 4.02 to the Canadian dollar, and 8.09 to the pound sterling.

What It Will Cost

Inflation in France was low during the late '80s, around 3% annually. Air and car travel in France can be expensive (gas prices are above average and tolls are payable on most highways). Train travel, though, is a good value.

Hotel and restaurant prices compensate for the expense of travel. Prices are above average in Paris, on the Riviera, and in the Alps during the skiing season (worst here in February). But even in these areas, you can find pleasant accommodations and excellent food at moderate prices. Hotel prices in the Loire Valley can be reasonable, but try to book well ahead in summer.

Taxes All taxes must be included in posted prices in France. The initials TTC (toutes taxes comprises—taxes included) sometimes appear on price lists but, strictly speaking, are superfluous. By law, restaurant and hotel prices must include 18.6% taxes and a service charge. If you discover that these have rematerialized as additional items on your bill, kick up a fuss.

Sample Prices The following are meant only as a general guide, and may change substantially as exchange rates fluctuate.

Daily newspaper: $1 French, $2 foreign; baguette: 65¢; cup of espresso in a café: $1.20; cup of coffee with milk: $2; half-liter carafe of table wine in budget restaurant: $5; glass of beer in café: $1.80; can of Coca-Cola: $1.20 in store, $3 in bar or restaurant; movie ticket: $8.

Passports and Visas

Americans All U.S. citizens are required to have a valid passport for entry into France. To obtain a new passport, apply in person; renewals can be obtained in person or by mail. First-time applicants should apply to one of the 13 U.S. Passport Agency offices at least five weeks before their departure date. In addition, local county courthouses, many state and probate courts, and some post offices accept passport applications. Necessary documents include (1) a completed passport application (Form DSP–11); (2) proof of citizenship (certified birth certificate issued by the Hall of Records of your state of birth or naturalization papers); (3) proof of identity (valid driver's license or state, military, or student ID card with your photograph and signature); (4) two recent, identical, two-inch-square photographs (black-and-white or color head shot with white or off-white background); and (5) a $65 application fee for a 10-year passport (those under 18 pay $40 for a five-year passport). You may pay with a check, money order, or an exact cash amount—no change is given. Passports are mailed to you in about 10–15 working days. To renew your passport by mail, send a completed Form DSP–82; two recent, identical passport photographs; your current passport (if it is less than 12 years old and was issued after your 16th birthday); and a check or money order for $55.

U.S. citizens do not need a visa to enter France for a period of 90 days. For further information, contact the Embassy of France, 4101 Reservoir Rd., NW, Washington, DC 20007, tel. 202/944–6000.

Canadians All Canadians are required to have a passport for entry into France. Send a completed application (available at any post office or passport office) to the Bureau of Passports (Suite 215, West Tower, Guy Favreau Complex, 200 René Lévesque Blvd. W., Montreal, Que. H2Z 1X4). Include $25, two photographs, a guarantor, and proof of Canadian citizenship. Applications may be made in person at the regional passport offices in Edmonton, Halifax, Montreal, Toronto, Vancouver, or Winnipeg. Passports are valid for five years and are nonrenewable.

Visas are not required of Canadian citizens to enter France. Obtain details regarding length of stay from the French Consulate or the French National Tourist Office.

Britons All British citizens need passports, for which applications are available from travel agencies or a main post office. Send the completed form to a regional Passport Office or apply in person at a main post office. You'll need two photographs and will be charged a £15 fee. The occasional tourist may opt for a British Visitors Passport. It is valid for one year, costs £7.50, and is nonrenewable. You'll need two passport photographs and identification. Apply at your local post office.

Visas are not required of British citizens entering France.

Customs and Duties

On Arrival There are two levels of duty-free allowance for travelers entering France: one for goods obtained (tax paid) within another European Community (EC) country and the other for goods obtained anywhere outside the EC or for goods purchased in a duty-free shop within the EC.

In the first category, you may import duty-free: 300 cigarettes or 150 cigarillos or 75 cigars or 400 grams of tobacco; five liters of table wine and (1) 1½ liters of alcohol over 22% (most spirits), (2) three liters of alcohol under 22% by volume (fortified or sparkling wine), or (3) three more liters of table wine; 90 milliliters of perfume; 375 milliliters of toilet water; and other goods to the value of 2,400 francs (620 francs for those under 15).

In the second category, you may import duty-free: 200 cigarettes or 100 cigarillos or 50 cigars or 250 grams of tobacco (these allowances are doubled if you live outside Europe); two liters of wine and (1) one liter of alcohol over 22% volume (most spirits), (2) two liters of alcohol under 22% volume (fortified or sparkling wine), or (3) two more liters of table wine; 60 milliliters of perfume; 250 milliliters of toilet water; and other goods to the value of 300 francs (150 francs for those under 15).

Any amount of French or foreign currency may be brought into France, but foreign currencies converted into francs may be reconverted into a foreign currency only up to the equivalent of 5,000 francs. Similarly, no more than 5,000 francs may be exported and no more than the equivalent of 2,000 francs in foreign currency may be exported.

On Departure U.S. residents who are bringing any foreign-made equipment,
U.S. Customs such as cameras, from home would be wise to carry the original receipt with them or register it with U.S. Customs before leaving home (Form 4457). Otherwise you may end up paying duty on your return. You may bring home duty-free up to $400 worth of foreign goods, as long as you have been out of the country for at least 48 hours and you haven't made an international trip in 30 days. Each member of the family is entitled to the same exemption, regardless of age, and exemptions may be pooled. For the next $1,000 worth of goods, a flat 10% rate is assessed; above $1,400, duties vary with the merchandise. Included for travelers 21 or older are one liter of alcohol, 100 cigars (non-Cuban), and 200 cigarettes. Only one bottle of perfume trademarked in the United States may be brought in. However, there is no duty on antiques or art over 100 years old. Anything exceeding these limits will be taxed at the port of entry and may be taxed again in the traveler's home state. Gifts valued at under $50 may be mailed to friends or relatives at home duty-free, but no more than one package per day may be sent to any one addressee and no perfumes costing more than $5, tobacco, or liquor may be mailed. For a complete run down on what returning residents may and may not bring back to the United States, obtain the free pamphlet "Know Before You Go" from U.S. Customs Service (1301 Constitution Ave., Washington, DC 20229).

Canadian Customs Exemptions for returning Canadians range from $20 to $300, depending on length of stay out of the country. For the $300 exemption, you must have been out of the country for one week. For any given year, you are allowed one $300 exemption. You may bring in duty-free up to 50 cigars, 200 cigarettes, 2.2 pounds of tobacco, and 40 ounces of liquor, provided these are declared in writing to customs on arrival and accompany the traveler in hand or in checked-through baggage. Personal gifts should be mailed as "Unsolicited Gift—Value under $40." Request the Canadian Customs brochure *I Declare* for further details.

U.K. Customs British residents have two different allowances: one for goods bought in a duty-free shop in France and the other for goods bought anywhere else in France.

In the first category, you may import duty-free: 200 cigarettes or 100 cigarillos or 50 cigars or 250 grams of tobacco (these allowances are doubled if you live outside Europe); two liters of table wine and (1) one liter of alcohol over 22% by volume (most spirits) or (2) two liters of alcohol under 22% by volume (fortified or sparkling wine) or (3) two more liters of table wine; 60 milliliters of perfume; 250 milliliters of toilet water; and other goods up to a value of £32, but no more than 50 liters of beer or 25 lighters.

In the second category, you may import duty-free: 300 cigarettes or 150 cigarillos or 75 cigars or 400 grams of tobacco; five liters of table wine and (1) 1½ liters of alcohol over 22% volume (most spirits) or (2) three liters of alcohol under 22% by volume (fortified or sparkling wine) or (3) three more liters of table wine; 90 milliliters of perfume; 375 milliliters of toilet water; and other goods to a value of £420, but no more than 50 liters of beer or 25 lighters.

No animals or pets of any kind may be brought into the United Kingdom without a lengthy quarantine. *The penalties are severe and strictly enforced.*

Traveling with Film

If your camera is new, shoot and develop a few rolls of film before leaving home. Pack some lens tissue and an extra battery for your built-in light meter. Film doesn't like hot weather, so if you're driving in summer, don't store it in the glove compartment or on the shelf under the rear window. Put it behind the front seat on the floor, on the side opposite the exhaust pipe.

On a plane trip, never pack unprocessed film in check-in luggage; if your bags are X-rayed, your pictures will be ruined. Always carry undeveloped film with you through security and ask to have it inspected by hand. (It helps to isolate your film in a plastic bag, ready for quick inspection.) Inspectors at U.S. airports are required by law to honor requests for hand inspection; abroad, you'll have to depend on the kindness of strangers.

The newer airport scanning machines used in all U.S. airports are safe for anything from 5 to 500 scans, depending on the speed of your film.

Language

The French study English for a minimum of four years at school (often longer) but to little general effect. English is widely understood in major tourist areas, however, and, no matter what the area, there should be at least one person in most hotels who can explain things to you if necessary. Be courteous and patient, and speak slowly: The French, after all, have plenty of other tourists and are not massively dependent for income on English-speaking visitors. And while it may sound cynical, remember that the French respond quicker to charm than to anything else.

Even if your own French is terrible, try to master a few words: The French are more cooperative when they think you're making at least an effort to speak their language. Basic vocabulary: *s'il vous plaît* (please), *merci* (thanks), *bonjour* (hello—until 6 PM), *bonsoir* (good evening), *au revoir* (goodbye), *comment ça va* (how do you do), *oui* (yes), *non* (no), *peut-être* (maybe), *les toilettes* (toilet), *l'addition* (bill/check), *où* (where), *anglais* (English), *je ne comprends pas* (I don't understand).

Refer to the French Vocabulary and Menu Guide at the back of the book.

Staying Healthy

There are no serious health risks associated with traveling in France. However, the Centers for Disease Control (CDC) in Atlanta cautions that most of southern Europe is in the "intermediate" range for risk of contracting traveler's diarrhea. Part of this risk may be attributed to an increased consumption of olive oil and wine, which can have a laxative effect on stomachs used to a different diet. The CDC also advises all international travelers to swim only in chlorinated swimming pools, unless they are certain the local beaches and freshwater lakes are not contaminated.

If you have a health problem that might require purchasing prescription drugs while in France, have your doctor write a prescription using the drug's generic name. Brand names vary widely from country to country.

The **International Association for Medical Assistance to Travelers (IAMAT)** is a worldwide association that publishes a list of approved physicians and clinics whose training meets British and American standards. For a list of French physicians and clinics that are part of this network, contact IAMAT (417 Center St., Lewiston, NY 14092, tel. 716/754–4883. **In Canada:** 40 Regal Rd., Guelph, Ontario N1K 1B5. **In Europe:** 57 Voirets, 1212 Grand-Lancy, Geneva, Switzerland). Membership is free.

Shots and Medications Inoculations are not needed to enter France. The American Medical Association recommends Pepto Bismol for minor cases of traveler's diarrhea.

Insurance

Travelers may seek insurance coverage in four areas: health and accident, loss of luggage, flight, and trip cancellation. Your first step is to review your existing health and home-owner policies: Some health insurance plans cover health expenses incurred while traveling, some major medical plans cover emergency transportation, and some home-owner policies cover the theft of luggage.

Health and Accident *In the United States* Several companies offer coverage, designed to supplement existing health insurance for travelers: These policies include 24-hour, worldwide medical referral and advice hotlines, emergency medical evacuation, medical insurance, and accidental death and dismemberment coverage.

Access America, Inc. (Box 11188, Richmond, VA 23230, tel. 800/334–7525 or 800/284–8300), a subsidiary of Blue Cross–Blue Shield; **Carefree Travel Insurance** (Box 310, 120 Mineola Blvd., Mineola, NY 11501, tel. 516/294–0220 or 800/323–3149); **International SOS Assistance** (Box 11568, Philadelphia, PA 19116, tel. 215/244–1500 or 800/523–8930); **Travel Guard International** (1145 Clark St., Stevens Point, WI 54481, tel. 715/345–0505 or 800/782–5151), underwritten by Transamerica Occidental Life Companies; and **Wallach and Company, Inc.** (Box 480, Middleburg, VA 22117–0480, tel. 703/687–3166 or 800/237–6615) offers such policies, differing only in their daily deductibles.

In the United Kingdom For advice on holiday insurance, contact the **Association of British Insurers** (51 Gresham St., London BC2V 7HQ, tel. 071/

600–3333) or **Europe Assistance** (252 High St., Croydon, Surrey CRO 1NF, tel. 081/680–1234).

Luggage The loss of luggage is usually covered as part of a comprehensive travel insurance package that includes personal accident, trip-cancellation, and sometimes default and bankruptcy insurance. Two companies offer comprehensive policies: **Access America, Inc.**, and **Travel Guard International** (*see* Health and Accident Insurance, *above*).

Trip-Cancellation and Flight Consider purchasing trip-cancellation insurance if you are traveling on a promotional or discounted ticket that does not allow changes or cancellations. You will then be covered if an emergency causes you to cancel or postpone your trip. Trip-cancellation insurance is usually included in combination-travel insurance packages available from most tour operators, travel agents, and insurance agents.

Flight insurance, which covers passengers in case of death or dismemberment, is often included in the price of a ticket when paid for with American Express, MasterCard, or other major credit cards.

Renting or Leasing Cars

Renting If you're flying into Paris or to a city in Provence or the Riviera and are planning to spend time there, save money by arranging to pick up your car in the city the day you depart; otherwise, arrange to pick up and return your car at the airport. You'll have to weigh the added expense of renting a car from a major company with an airport office against the savings on a car from a budget company with offices in town. You could waste precious hours trying to locate the budget company in return for only a small financial savings. If you're arriving and departing from different airports, look for a one-way car rental with no return fees. If you're traveling to more than one country, make sure your rental contract permits you to take the car across borders and that the insurance policy covers you in every country you visit. Be prepared to pay more for cars with automatic transmissions. Since they are not as readily available as those with manual transmissions, reserve them well in advance.

Rental rates vary widely, depending on the size and model, the number of days you use the car, insurance coverage, and whether special drop-off fees are imposed. In many cases, rates quoted include unlimited free mileage and standard liability protection. Not included are Collision Damage Waiver (CDW), which eliminates your deductible payment if you have an accident, personal accident insurance, gasoline, and European Value-Added Taxes (VAT). The VAT on car rentals in France is among the highest in Europe.

Driver's licenses issued in the United States and Canada are valid in France. You may also take out an International Driving Permit before you leave to smooth out difficulties if you have an accident or as an additional piece of identification. Permits are available for a small fee through local offices of the **American Automobile Association** (AAA) and the **Canadian Automobile Association** (CAA) or from their main offices (AAA, 1000 AAA Dr., Heathrow, FL 32746–0001, tel. 800/336–4357; CAA, 2 Carlton St., Toronto, Ontario M5B 1K4, tel. 416/964–3002).

It's best to arrange a car rental before you leave. You won't save money by waiting until you arrive in France, and you may find that the type of car you want is not available at the last minute. Rental companies usually charge according to the exchange rate of the dollar at the time the car is returned or when the credit-card payment is processed. Two companies with special programs to help you hedge against the falling dollar, by guaranteeing advertised rates if you pay in advance, are **Budget Rent-a-Car** (3350 Boyington St., Carrollton, TX 75006, tel. 800/527–0700) and **Connex Travel International** (23 N. Division St., Peekskill, NY 10566, tel. 800/333–3949). Other budget rental companies serving Europe include **Europe by Car** (1 Rockefeller Plaza, New York, NY 10020, tel. 212/245–1713, 800/223–1516, or 800/252–9401 in CA), **Auto Europe** (Box 1097 Sharps Wharf, Camden, ME 04843, tel. 800/223–5555), **Foremost Euro-Car** (5430 Van Nuys Blvd., Van Nuys, CA 91401, tel. 800/272–3299), and **Kemwel** (106 Calvert St. Harrison, NY 10528, tel. 800/678–0678). Others with European rentals include **Avis** (tel. 800/331–1212), **Hertz** (tel. 800/654–3131), **National or Europcar** (tel. 800/227–7368), and **Thrifty** (tel. 800/367–2277).

In the United Kingdom, there are offices of **Avis** (Trident House, Station Rd., Hayes Middlesex UB3 4DJ, tel. 081/848–8765); **Hertz** (Radnor House, 1272 London Rd., London SW16 4XW, tel. 081/679–1799); and **Europcar Ltd.** (Bushey House, High St., Bushey, Watford WD2 1RE, tel. 081/950–4080).

Leasing For trips of 21 days or more, you may save money by leasing a car. With the leasing arrangement, you are technically buying a car and then selling it back to the manufacturer after you've used it. You receive a factory-new car, tax-free, with international registration and extensive insurance coverage. Rates vary with the make and model of the car and the length of time it is used. Car-leasing programs in France are offered by Renault, Citroën, and Peugeot. Delivery is free to downtown Paris and to the airports in Paris. There is a small fee for deliveries to other parts of France. Before you go, compare long-term rental rates with leasing rates. Remember to add taxes and insurance costs to the car rentals, something you don't have to worry about with leasing. Companies that offer leasing arrangements include **Kemwel, Europe by Car,** and **Auto Europe,** all listed above.

Rail Passes

The **French Flexipass** (formerly the **France-Vacances Rail Pass)** is a good value for those who plan to do a lot of traveling by train. The Flexipass allows you to stagger your train travel time instead of having to use it all at once. For example, the four-day pass ($175 in first class, $125 in second) can be used on any four days within a one-month period. Travelers may also add up to five additional days of travel for $38 a day in first class or $27 a day in second class.

You must buy the French Flexipass before you leave for France. It is obtainable through travel agents or through **Rail Europe** (226–230 Westchester Ave., White Plains, NY 10604, tel. 914/682–5172 or 800/345–1990).

The **EurailPass,** valid for unlimited first-class train travel through 20 countries, including France, is an excellent value if you plan to travel around the Continent. The ticket is available for periods of 15 days ($430), 21 days ($550), one month ($680), two months ($920), and three months ($1,150). For two or more people traveling together, a 15-day rail pass costs $340. Between April 1 and September 30, you need a minimum of three in your group to get this discount. For those younger than 26 years old (on the first day of travel), there is the **Eurail Youthpass,** for one or two months of unlimited second-class train travel at $470 and $640. The **BritFrance Rail Pass** allows you to travel for any 5 of 15 days in France and Britain (including Channel crossing by Hovercraft) for $249 (second class) or $335 (first class), or for any 10 days in a 30-day period ($385/$505). You can obtain the pass from travel agencies or Rail Europe.

For travelers who like to spread out their train journeys, there is the **Eurail Flexipass.** With the 15-day Flexipass ($280), travelers get 5 days of unlimited first-class train travel but can spread that travel out over 15 days; a 21-day pass gives you 9 days of travel ($450), and a one-month pass gives you 14 days ($610).

The EurailPass is available only if you live outside Europe or North Africa. The pass must be bought from an authorized agent before you leave for Europe. Apply through your travel agent or through **Rail Europe** (address above).

Student and Youth Travel

The **International Student Identity Card (ISIC)** entitles students to youth rail passes, special fares on local transportation, intra-European student charter flights, and discounts at sports events, museums, theaters, and many other attractions. The ISIC is available upon presentation of a valid college ID, in the United States for $15 from the Council on International Education Exchange (CIEE, 205 E. 42nd St., 16th floor, New York, NY 10017, tel. 212/661–1414 or 800/438–2643), in Canada, for $13 from Travel Cuts (187 College St., Toronto, Ont. M5T 1P7, tel. 416/979–2406), and in the United Kingdom for £5 from any student union or travel company. Cards purchased in the United States also buy $3,000 in emergency medical insurance and reimbursement of $100 a day for up to 60 days of hospital coverage.

You need only be under 26 to apply for an **International Youth Card** (IYC), issued by the Federation of International Youth Travel Organizations (FIYTO, Delta Budget Rejser, Vesterbrogade 26, 1620 Copenhagen V, Denmark, tel. 45/31311112). Providing benefits similar to those of the ISIC card, it is available in the United States for $15 from CIEE (*see abive*), in Canada for $26.75 (including IYHF membership, *see below*) from the Canadian Hostelling Association (CHA, 1600 James Naismith Dr., Suite 608, Gloucester, Ontario K1B 5N4, tel. 613/748–5638), and in the United Kingdom for 4£ from any student union or student travel company.

An **International Youth Hostel Federation Membership Card** (IYHF) is the key to more than 6,000 hostel locations in 70 countries worldwide; the sex-segregated, dormitory-style sleeping quarters, including some for families, go for $7 to $20 a night per person. Members can also get reductions on rail and bus travel around the world and handbooks detailing membership benefits. You can join in the United States through American Youth Hostels (AYH, Box 37613, Washington, DC 20013, tel. 202/783–6161), in Canada through the CHA (*see above*), and in the United Kingdom through the Youth Hostel Association of England and Wales (Trevelyan House, 8 St. Stephen's Hill, St. Albans, Herts. AL1 2DY, tel. 727/55215). First-year membership cost is $25 for adults 18 through 54, $10 for those under 18, $15 for those 55 and over, and $35 for families in the United States; $26.75 in Canada (including IYC cost); and £9 for adults in the United Kingdom, with children under 16 free if both parents are members.

Economical **bicycle tours** for small groups of adventurous, energetic travelers of all ages are another popular AYH student travel service. For information on these and other AYH services and publications, contact AYH at the address listed above.

Council Travel, a CIEE subsidiary, is the foremost U.S. student travel agency, specializing in low-cost charters and serving as the exclusive U.S. agent for many student airfare bargains and student tours. CIEE's 72-page *Student Travel Catalog* and *Council Charter* brochure are available free from any Council Travel office in the United States (enclose $1 for postage if ordering by mail). In addition to CIEE headquarters (205 E. 42nd St., New York, NY 10017) and a branch office (35 W. 8th St. in New York, NY 10009), there are Council Travel offices in Tempe, AZ; Berkeley, La Jolla, Long Beach, Los Angeles, San Diego, and San Francisco, CA; Chicago, IL; Amherst, Boston, and Cambridge, MA; Portland, OR; Providence, RI; Austin and Dallas, TX; and Seattle, WA, among other cities.

Students who would like to work abroad should contact **CIEE's Work Abroad Department** (205 E. 42nd St., New York, NY 10017, tel. 212/661–1414, ext. 1130). The council arranges various types of paid and voluntary work experiences overseas for up to six months. CIEE also sponsors study programs in Europe and publishes many books of interest to the student traveler. These books include *Work, Study, Travel Abroad: The Whole World Handbook* ($12.95), *Volunteer! The Comprehensive Guide to Voluntary Service in the U.S. and Abroad* ($8.95), and *The Teenager's Guide to Travel, Study, and Adventure Abroad* ($11.95); add $1.50 (book-rate) or $3 (first-class) postage for each title.

The Information Center at the **Institute of International Education** (IIE) has reference books, foreign university catalogues, study-abroad brochures, and other materials that may be consulted by students and nonstudents alike free of charge. The Information Center (809 UN Plaza, New York, NY 10017, tel. 212/883–8200) is open from 10 AM to 4 PM weekdays and until 7 PM Wednesday evenings. It is not open on weekends or holidays.

IIE administers a variety of grant and study programs offered by U.S. and foreign organizations, and publishes a well-known annual series of study-abroad guides, including *Academic Year Abroad, Vacation Study Abroad,* and *Study in the United Kingdom and Ireland.* The institute also publishes *Teaching Abroad,* a book of employment and study opportunities overseas for U.S. teachers. For a current list of IIE publications with prices and ordering information, write to Publications Service, Institute of International Education (809 UN Plaza,

New York, NY 10017). Books must be purchased by mail or in person; telephone orders are not accepted.

General information on IIE's programs and services is available from its regional offices in Atlanta, Chicago, Denver, Houston, San Francisco, and Washington, DC.

For information on the **Eurail Youthpass,** *see* Rail Passes, above.

Traveling with Children

Publications   *Family Travel Times* is an 8–12-page newsletter published 10 times a year by **TWYCH** (Travel with Your Children, 45 W. 18th St., 7th Floor Tower, New York, NY 10011, tel. 212/206–0688). Subscription includes access to back issues and a weekly opportunity to call in for specific advice.

Traveling with Children—And Enjoying It ($11.95; Globe Pequot Press, Box Q, Chester, CT 06412) offers tips on how to cut costs, keep kids busy, eat out, reduce jet lag, and pack effectively.

Family Travel **American Institute for Foreign Study** (AIFS, 102 Greenwich
Organizations Ave., Greenwich, CT 06830, tel. 203/869–9090) offers family vacation programs in France for high school- and college-age students, as well as interested adults. Programs for high school students are handled by **Educational Travel Division, American Council for International Studies** (19 Bay State Rd., Boston, MA 02215, tel. 617/236–2015 or 800/825–2437). For information on programs for college students, contact AIFS (102 Greenwich Ave., Greenwich, CT 06830, tel. 203/869–9090).

Families Welcome! (Box 16398, Chapel Hill, NC 27516, tel. 800/ 326–0724) is a travel agency that arranges French tours brimming with family-sensitive choices and activities. Another travel arranger that understands families' needs (and can even set up short-term rentals) is **The French Experience** (370 Lexington Ave., New York, NY 10017, tel. 212/986–3800).

Hotels The **Novotel** hotel chain allows up to two children under 15 to stay free in their parents' room. Many Novotel properties have playgrounds. (For international reservations, call 800/221– 4542). **Sofitel** hotels offer a free second room for children during July and August and over the Christmas holidays. (For international reservations, call 800/221–4542.) **Club Med** (40 W. 57th St., New York, NY 10019, tel. 800/258–2633) has a "Baby Club" (from age four months) at its resort in Chamonix; "Mini Clubs" (for ages four to six or eight, depending on the resort), and "Kids Clubs" (for ages eight and up during school holidays) at all its resort villages in Provence and the Riviera. In general, supervised activities are scheduled all day long. Some clubs are only French-speaking, so check first.

Villa Rentals **At Home Abroad, Inc.,** 405 E. 56th St., Suite 6H, New York, NY 10022, tel. 212/421–9165. **Villas International,** 605 Market St., Suite 510, San Francisco, CA 94105, tel. 415/281–0910 or 800/ 221–2260. **Hideaways, Int'l.,** Box 1270, Littleton, MA 01460, tel. 508/486–8955. **B. & D. de Vogue,** 1830 S. Mooney Blvd. 113, Visalia, CA 93277, tel. 209/733–7119 or 800/727–4748. **Vacances en Campagne,** Box 297, Falls Village, CT 06031, tel. 203/824– 5155 or 800/553–5405.

Home Exchange Exchanging homes is a surprisingly low-cost way to enjoy a vacation abroad, especially a long one. The largest home-exchange service, **Intervac U.S./International Home Exchange Service** (Box 590504, San Francisco, CA 94159, tel. 415/435–3497 or 800/756–4663) publishes three directories a year. Membership costs $45 and entitles you to one listing and all three directories. **Loan-a-Home** (2 Park La., Apt. 6E, Mount Vernon, NY 10552, tel. 914/664–7640) is popular with the academic community on sabbatical and with businesspeople on temporary assignments. Although there's no annual membership fee or charge for listing your home, one directory and a supplement cost $35.

Getting There On international flights, children under two not occupying a seat pay 10% of the adult fare. Various discounts apply to children 2 to 12 years of age. Regulations about infant travel on airplanes are in the process of being changed. Until they do, however, if you want to be sure your infant is secure and can travel in his or her own safety seat, you must buy a separate ticket and bring your own infant car seat. (Check with the airline in advance; certain seats aren't allowed.) Some airlines allow babies to travel in their own car seats at no charge if there's a spare seat available, otherwise safety seats are stored and the child has to be held by a parent. (For the booklet *Child/Infant Safety Seats Acceptable for Use in Aircraft*, write to the Federal Aviation Administration, APA-200, 800 Independence Ave. SW, Washington, DC 20591, tel. 202/267–3479.) If you opt to hold your baby on your lap, do so with the infant outside the seat belt so he or she doesn't get crushed in case of a sudden stop.

Also inquire about special children's meals or snacks. The February 1990 and 1992 issues of *Family Travel Times* include *TWYCH's Airline Guide*, which contains a rundown of the children's services offered by 46 airlines.

Getting Around The **French National Railways** (SNCF) accommodates family travel by allowing children under four to travel free (provided they don't occupy a seat) and by allowing children four to 11 to travel at half fare. There is also the *Carte Kiwi*, costing 395 francs, which allows children under 16 and up to four accompanying adults to travel at half fare.

Baby-sitting Services Check with the hotel concierge for recommended child-care arrangements.

Miscellaneous Contact the **CIDJ** (Centre d'Information et de Documentation pour la Jeunesse, 101 quai Branly, 75015 Paris, tel. 45–67–35–85) for information about activities and events for youngsters in France.

Hints for Disabled Travelers

In France Facilities for the disabled in France are better than average. The French government is doing much to ensure that public facilities provide for disabled visitors, and it has produced an excellent booklet—*Tourists Quand Même*—with an English glossary and easily understood symbols detailing, region by region, facilities available to the disabled in transportation systems and museums and monuments. The booklet is available from French national tourist offices and from the main Paris Tourist Office, or from the **Comité National Français de Liaison**

pour la Réadaptation des Handicapés (38 blvd. Raspail, 75007 Paris, tel. 45–44–33–23).

A number of monuments, hotels, and museums—especially those constructed within the past decade—are equipped with ramps, elevators, or special toilet facilities. Lists of regional hotels include a symbol to indicate which hotels have rooms that are accessible to the disabled. Similarly, the SNCF has special cars on some trains that have been reserved exclusively for the handicapped and can arrange for wheelchair-bound passengers to be escorted on and off trains and assisted in catching connecting trains (the latter service must be requested in advance).

A helpful organization in Paris is the **Association des Paralysés de France** (17 blvd. Auguste-Blanqui, 75013 Paris, tel. 40–78–69–00), which publishes a useful hotel list.

Free baby-sitting for physically and mentally disabled children is provided by the **Fondation Claude Pompidou** (42 rue du Louvre, 75001 Paris, tel. 45–08–45–15; phone between 2 and 6). Services are available at all times.

In the U.S. Tours that are especially designed for disabled travelers generally parallel those for able-bodied travelers, albeit at a more leisurely pace. For a complete list of tour operators who arrange such travel, write to the **Society for the Advancement of Travel for the Handicapped** (347 Fifth Ave., Suite 610, New York, NY 10016, tel. 212/447–7288, fax 212/725–8253). Annual membership costs $45, or $25 for senior citizens and students. Send a stamped, self-addressed envelope for information on specific destinations. Information is available to nonmembers for $3.

Moss Rehabilitation Hospital (1200 W. Tabor Rd., Philadelphia, PA 19141–3099, tel. 215/456–9603) answers inquiries regarding specific cities and countries and provides toll-free telephone numbers for airlines with special lines for the hard-of-hearing and, again, listings of selected tour operators.

The **Information Center for Individuals with Disabilities** (Fort Point Pl., 1st floor, 27–43 Wormwood St., Boston, MA 02210, tel. 617/727–5540) offers useful problem-solving assistance, including lists of travel agents that specialize in tours for the disabled.

Mobility International USA (Box 3551, Eugene, OR 97403, tel. 503/343–1284) has information on accommodations, organized study, and so forth around the world, and publishes *A World of Options for the 90's*, a guide to travel for people with disabilities ($16). Annual membership is $15.

The Itinerary (Box 2012, Bayonne, NJ 07002, tel. 201/858–3400) is a bimonthly travel magazine for the disabled.

Nautilus Tours (5435 Donna Ave., Tarzana, CA 91356, tel. 818/343–6339) has for nine years operated international trips and cruises for the disabled. **Travel Industry and Disabled Exchange** (TIDE, at the same address, tel. 818/368–5648), an industry-based organization with a $15 annual membership fee, provides a quarterly newsletter and information on travel agencies and tours.

Twin Peaks Press (Box 129, Vancouver, WA 98666, tel. 206/694–2462 or 800/637–2256) publishes books for the disabled, among them *The Directory of Travel Agencies for the Disabled*

($19.95), listing over 300 agencies worldwide; *Wheelchair Vagabond* ($14.95), offering tips from personal travel experiences; *Travel for the Disabled* ($19.95), which details guidebooks and facilities for the disabled; and *The Directory of Accessible Van Rentals* ($9.95), for campers and RV travelers worldwide. Twin Peaks' "Traveling Nurse's Network" provides RNs to accompany disabled travelers.

Hints for Older Travelers

The **American Association of Retired Persons** (AARP, 601 E St. NW, Washington, DC 20049, tel. 202/434–2277) has a program for independent travelers: *The Purchase Privilege Program,* which offers discounts on hotels, airfare, car rentals, and sightseeing. The AARP can also arrange group tours, including apartment living in Europe. AARP members must be 50 or older. Annual dues are $5 per person or per couple.

When using an AARP or other identification card, ask for a reduced hotel rate at the time you make your reservation, not when you check out. At participating restaurants, show your card to the maitre d' before you're seated since discounts may be limited to certain set menus, days, or hours. When renting a car, be sure to ask about special promotional rates that might offer greater savings than the available discount.

Elderhostel (75 Federal St., 3rd floor, Boston, MA 02210, tel. 617/426–7788) is an innovative, low-cost educational program for people 60 and older. Participants live in dorms on some 1,600 campuses around the world. Mornings are devoted to lectures and seminars, afternoons to sightseeing and field trips. All-inclusive fees for two- to three-week international trips, including room, board, tuition, and round-trip transportation, range from $1,800 to $4,500.

Travel Industry and Disabled Exchange (TIDE, 5435 Donna Ave., Tarzana, CA 91356, tel. 818/368–5648) is an industry-based organization with a $15 per person annual membership fee. Members receive a quarterly newsletter and information on travel agencies and tours.

National Council of Senior Citizens (1331 F St. NW, Washington, DC 20004, tel. 202/347–8800) is a nonprofit advocacy group with some 5,000 local clubs across the country. Annual membership is $12 per person or per couple. Members receive a monthly newspaper with travel information and an identification card for reduced-rate hotels and car rentals.

Mature Outlook (6001 N. Clark St., Chicago, IL 60660, tel. 800/ 336–6330), a subsidiary of Sears Roebuck & Co., is a travel club for people over 50, offering hotel and motel discounts and a bimonthly newsletter. Annual membership is $9.95 per couple. Instant membership is available at participating Holiday Inns.

In France Senior citizens (men over 62 and women over 60) enjoy reduced museum admission (usually 50%) and cheap train tickets (the **Carte Vermeil,** available at stations throughout France; the Carte Vermeil costs 165 francs a year and entitles the holder to discounts of up to 50%, depending on when you travel). Senior citizens should keep their passport or an identification card with them at all times.

Further Reading

A summary of recent social, political, and economic developments is provided by John Ardagh's *France Today* (Penguin). *Portraits of France* (Little Brown), by Robert Daly; *Two Towns in Provence* (Vintage), by M.F.K. Fisher; and *Provence* (The Ecco Press), by Ford Madox Ford, all combine personal and historical reminiscences of Provence, with Ardagh's book including essays on cities of the Riviera. Peter Mayle's *Toujours Provence* and *A Year in Provence* (Knopf/Vintage) also provide detailed personal portraits of Provence. Another author whose descriptive powers seldom disappoint is Emile Zola, and many of his books are set in Provence.

Books about French wine are numerous, but Steven Spurrier's pocket-size *French Country Wines* (Putnam) is unusual in its thorough treatment of lesser-known (and often good-value) wines. Architecture buffs should read Henri Focillon's *The Art of the West* (Cornell University Press) for a thoughtfully illustrated, scholarly exposé of Romanesque and Gothic architecture.

Arriving and Departing

Since the air routes between North America and France are among the world's most heavily traveled, passengers can choose from many different airlines and fares. But fares change with stunning rapidity, so consult your travel agent on which bargains are currently available.

From the U.S. by Plane

Be certain to distinguish among (1) nonstop flights—no changes, no stops; (2) direct flights—no changes but one or more stops; and (3) connecting flights—two or more planes, one or more stops.

Airports and Airlines The U.S. airlines that serve France are **TWA** (tel. 800/892–4141), **American Airlines** (tel. 800/433–7300), and **Delta** (tel. 800/241–4141). All fly to Paris's Charles de Gaulle (Roissy) Airport (tel. 48–62–22–80) and Orly (tel. 49–75–52–52). Delta also flies to Nice.

Flying Time to Nice From New York: 7¾ hours. From Chicago: 10 hours. From Los Angeles: 13¼ hours.

Discount Flights The major airlines offer a range of tickets that can increase the price of any given seat by more than 300%, depending on the day of purchase. As a rule, the further in advance you buy the ticket, the less expensive it is and the greater the penalty (up to 100%) for canceling. Check with the airlines for details.

The best buy is not necessarily an **APEX** (advance-purchase) ticket on one of the major airlines. APEX tickets carry certain restrictions: They must be bought in advance (usually 21 days); they restrict your travel, usually with a minimum stay of seven days and a maximum of 90; and they penalize you for changes—voluntary or not—in your travel plans. But if you can work around these drawbacks (and most travelers can), they are among the best-value fares available.

Travelers who are willing to put up with a few restrictions and inconveniences in exchange for a substantially reduced fare may be interested in flying as **air couriers.** A courier must accompany shipments between designated points. There are several sources of information on courier deals, including (1) a telephone directory that lists courier companies by the cities to which they fly (send $5 and a self-addressed, stamped, business-size envelope to Pacific Data Sales Publishing, 2554 Lincoln Blvd., Suite 275–I, Marina Del Rey, CA 92091) and (2) *A Simple Guide to Courier Travel* (send $15.95 to Box 2394, Lake Oswego, OR 97035. For more information, call 800/222–3599).

Charter flights offer the lowest fares but often depart only on certain days, and seldom on time. Though you may be able to arrive at one city and return from another, you may lose all or most of your money if you cancel your ticket. Don't sign up for a charter flight unless you've checked with a travel agent about the reputation of the packager. It's particularly important to know the packager's policy concerning refunds if a flight is canceled. One of the most popular charter operators to Europe is **Council Charter** (tel. 212/661–0311 or 800/800–8222), a division of **CIEE** (Council on International Educational Exchange). Other companies advertise in the Sunday travel sections of newspapers.

Somewhat more expensive—but up to 50% below the cost of APEX fares—are tickets purchased through companies, known as **consolidators,** that buy blocks of tickets on scheduled airlines and sell them at wholesale prices. Here again, you may lose all or most of your money if you change your plans, but at least you will be on a regularly scheduled flight with less risk of cancellation than a charter. Once you've made your reservation, call the airline to make sure you're confirmed. Among the best-known consolidators are **UniTravel** (Box 12485, St. Louis, MO 63132, tel. 314/569–2501 or 800/325–2222) and **Access International** (101 W. 31st St., Suite 1104, New York, NY 10001, tel. 212/465–0707 or 800/825–3633). Others advertise in the Sunday travel sections of newspapers as well.

Yet another option is to join a **travel club** that offers special discounts to its members. Three such organizations are **Moment's Notice** (425 Madison Ave., New York, NY 10017, tel. 212/486–0500); **Discount Travel International** (114 Forrest Ave., Narberth, PA 19072, tel. 215/668–7184 or 800/334–9294); and **Worldwide Discount Travel Club** (1674 Meridian Ave., Miami Beach, FL 33139, tel. 305/534–2082). These cut-rate tickets should be compared with APEX tickets on the major airlines.

Enjoying the Flight As the air on a plane is dry, it helps, while flying, to drink a lot of nonalcoholic liquids; drinking alcohol contributes to jet lag, as does eating heavy meals on board. Feet swell at high altitudes, so it's a good idea to remove your shoes while in flight. Sleepers usually prefer window seats to curl up against; those who like to move about the cabin should ask for aisle seats. Bulkhead seats (located in the front row of each cabin) have more legroom, but seat trays are attached to the arms of your seat rather than to the back of the seat in front. Bulkhead seats are generally reserved for the elderly, the disabled, or parents traveling with babies.

Smoking Smoking is banned on all scheduled routes within the 48 contiguous states; within the states of Hawaii and Alaska; to and from the U.S. Virgin Islands and Puerto Rico; and on flights of fewer than six hours to and from Hawaii and Alaska. The rule applies to the domestic legs of all foreign routes but does not affect international flights.

It is best to request a no-smoking seat at the time you book your ticket. If a U.S. airline representative tells you there are no seats available in the no-smoking section, insist on one: Department of Transportation regulations require U.S. flag carriers to find seats for all nonsmokers on the day of the flight, provided they meet check-in time restrictions. On foreign carriers, ask for a seat far from the smoking section.

From the U.S. by Ship

The *Queen Elizabeth 2 (QE2)* is the only ocean liner that makes regular transatlantic crossings. However, the *Vistafjord* of the Cunard Line sails between Fort Lauderdale, Florida, and Marseille, France, in repositioning crossings. These crossings occur when cruise ships are taken to or from North America and Europe as one season ends and another begins. Some sail straight across, often at reduced rates to passengers. Others stop at several ports of call before heading to open sea. Arrangements can be made to cruise one way and fly one way. Because itineraries can change at the last minute, check with the cruise lines for the latest information.

Cunard Line (555 Fifth Ave., New York, NY 10017, tel. 800/221–4770; in NY 212/880–7545) operates four ships, including the *QE2* and *Vistafjord*. The *QE2* makes regular crossings from April through December, between Baltimore, Boston, and New York City and Southampton, England. Arrangements for the *QE2* can include one-way airfare. Cunard Line offers fly/cruise packages and pre- and postland packages. For the European cruise season, ports of call include Southhampton; Madeira; Marseille; Hamburg, Germany; Genoa, Rome, Venice, and Naples, Italy; Monte Carlo, Monaco; Malaga, Spain; Piraeus (Athens), Greece; Copenhagen, Denmark; and Stockholm, Sweden. Ports of call vary with the ship.

Royal Viking Line (750 Battery St., San Francisco, CA 94111, tel. 800/634–8000) has three ships that cruise out of European ports. Two of the ships make repositioning crossings between Fort Lauderdale, Florida, and Lisbon, Portugal. Fly/cruise packages are available. Major ports of call, depending on the ship, are Copenhagen, Denmark; Stockholm, Sweden; Bergen, Norway; Hamburg, Germany; Leningrad, Russia; Barcelona, Spain; Venice, Italy; Dubrovnik, Yugoslavia; Villefranche, France; Corfu, Greece; and Lisbon, Portugal.

Check the travel pages of your Sunday newspaper for other cruise ships that sail to Europe.

From the U.K. by Plane, Car, Train, and Bus

By Plane Some of the airlines operating between the United Kingdom and France are **Air France** (tel. 081/742–6600), **British Airways** (tel. 081/897–4000), and **Caledonian Airways** (tel. 0293/36321), the charter division of British Airways.

The route from London to Paris (journey time: one hour) is the busiest in Europe, with up to 17 flights daily from Heathrow

(Air France/British Airways) and four or five from Gatwick (Air France), all to Charles de Gaulle (also known as Roissy). There are also regular flights—geared mainly to business-people—from the new London City Airport in the Docklands; direct flights to Paris from several regional U.K. airports, including Manchester, Birmingham, Glasgow, Edinburgh, and Southampton; and flights from London to Nice, Lyon, Bordeaux, Marseille, Clermont-Ferrand, Caen, Quimper, Nantes, Montpellier, and Toulouse, as well as from Manchester to Nice. Remember, though, flying to France is often absurdly expensive. Charter flights (contact **Nouvelles Frontières**, 1–2 Hanover St., London W1R 9WB, tel. 071/629–7772), including Caledonian Airways' service between Gatwick and Beauvais, north of Paris, offer the best value.

By Car   There is no shortage of Channel crossings from England to France; all boats (and Hovercraft) welcome motor vehicles. The quickest and most frequent routes are between Dover and Calais/Boulogne: P & O runs up to 21 daily services. The Dover–Calais journey time is 75 minutes and the Dover–Boulogne, 100 minutes.

Each of the other routes has geographic advantages to offset its comparative slowness. Ramsgate–Dunkirk (Sally Line: 2½ hours) offers excellent restaurant and duty-free facilities, plus minimum fuss at port terminals; Newhaven–Dieppe (Sealink: 4½ hours) lands you in pretty Normandy; Portsmouth–Caen/St-Malo (Brittany Ferries: six hours) can take you either to Brittany (St-Malo) or within striking distance of Paris (Caen); while Portsmouth–Le Havre/Cherbourg (P & O: six hours), Plymouth–Roscoff (Brittany Ferries: eight hours), and Poole/Weymouth–Cherbourg (Brittany Ferries: eight hours) all cater to drivers from Wales and southwestern England.

The Ramsgate–Dunkirk service operates several times daily, the rest at least once a day (Weymouth–Cherbourg summer only). The Hoverspeed crossings between Dover and Boulogne/Calais take just over half an hour but are suspended during heavy winds and, therefore, unreliable in winter. Whichever route you choose, it is advisable to book ahead. Prices and timetables vary according to season, time of day, and length of stay, so contact the relevant ferry operator for details: **Sealink** (tel. 0233/647047), **Sally Line** (tel. 0843/595566), **Brittany Ferries** (tel. 0705/827701), **P & O** (tel. 081/575–8555), and **Hoverspeed** (tel. 0304/240241).

In mid-1993 cars should be able to reach France through the Channel Tunnel, aboard special double-decker trains that will shuttle between Folkestone and Sangatte every 15 minutes.

By Train   Until the Channel Tunnel is opened in mid-1993, as scheduled (journey time will be slashed to 3½ hours), traveling by train from London to Paris and other French cities means hassle—in the form of purposeless waiting, lengthy lines, and a pervading air of either dilapidation (British Rail) or indifference (French officialdom). If there are no unforeseen delays, the journeys from London to Paris via Dover or Folkestone take around seven hours. The trip via Newhaven–Dieppe—offering the cheapest prices to those aged under 26—takes nine hours. Check train/ferry prices with Sealink/British Rail, since there are numerous variations, depending on the time, season, crossing, and length of travel. The faster and more convenient Hovercraft service via Dover–Boulogne takes under six hours, but remember that Hovercraft are more affected by high winds and are relatively expensive (around £46 each way, although five-day minivacations are a good value at just around £60). There are also good-value five-day trips to such destinations as Lyon, Avignon, and Cannes. For more information, contact Sealink or British Rail.

Paris is the hub of the French train system and a change, both of train and station, is often necessary if your destination lies farther afield. There are, however, direct trains from London to Strasbourg, Lyon, the Alps, the Riviera, and the Pyrenees.

By Bus If you prefer bus to train travel, a London-to-Paris bus journey can be a rewarding experience (and costs only a little over £50 round-trip). **Eurolines** (tel. 071/730–0202), the international affiliate of **National Express,** runs four daily *Citysprint* buses in summer from Victoria Coach Station to the rue Lafayette in Paris near the Gare du Nord; these buses use the Hovercraft crossing, and the journey time is around 7½ hours. Three daily buses from Victoria to the Porte de la Villette on the outskirts of Paris use traditional ferries for the Channel crossing and take a bit longer (9 to 10 hours).

Eurolines has buses to the Riviera, leaving Victoria three times a week for such resorts as Nice and Cannes. The round-trip fare to Cannes is £99.

In addition, Eurolines (tel. 071/730–0202) operates an express service that runs overnight to Grenoble, where there are connecting services to Nice and Marseille (return trip to Nice costs about £99).

Staying in Provence and the Riviera

Getting Around Provence and the Riviera

By Plane France's domestic airline service is called **Air Inter,** with flights from Paris to all major cities and many interregional flights. For long journeys—from Paris to the Riviera, for instance—air travel is a time saver, though train travel is always much cheaper. Most domestic flights from Paris leave from **Orly Airport** (tel. 49–75–15–15). For details, check with the local airport or call Air Inter (tel. 45–46–90–00).

By Train The SNCF is generally recognized as Europe's best national train service: It's fast, punctual, comfortable, and comprehensive. The high-speed TGVs, or *Train à Grande Vitesse* (average 255 kph/160 mph on the Lyon/southeast line) is the best domestic train, operating between Paris and Lyon/Switzerland/the Riviera. As with other main-line trains, you may need to pay a small supplement when taking a TGV at peak hours. Unlike other trains, the TGV *always* requires a seat reservation—easily obtained at the ticket window or from an automatic machine. Seat reservations are reassuring but seldom necessary on other main-line French trains, except at certain busy holiday times.

If you are traveling from Paris (or any other station terminus), get to the station half an hour before departure to ensure that you'll have a good seat. The majority of intercity trains in France consist of open-plan cars and are known as *Corail* trains. They are clean and extremely comfortable, even in second class. Trains on regional branch lines are currently being spruced up but lag behind in style and quality. The food in French trains can be good, but it's poor value for the money.

It is possible to get from one end of France to the other without resorting to overnight train travel. Otherwise you have the choice between high-priced *wagons-lits* (sleeping cars) and affordable (around 80 francs) *couchettes* (bunks), six to a compartment (sheet and pillow provided). Special summer night trains from Paris to the Riviera, geared to younger people, are equipped with disco and bar to enable you to dance and talk the night away.

Rail Europe has introduced a series of "Rail-and-Drive" packages that combine rail- and rental car–travel. The most extensive coverage is offered with the Eurail Drive pass, good for four train and three Hertz rental car days within a 21-day period. The cost is $269 per person (for two people traveling together). "France Rail 'N Drive" offers four rail days and three car days within one month for $159–$255 per person.

Fares Various reduced fares are available. Senior citizens (over 60) and young people (under 26) are eligible for the **Carte Vermeil** (165 francs) and **Carrissimo** (190 francs for four trips, 350 for eight) respectively, with proof of identity and two passport photos. The SNCF offers 50% reductions during "blue" periods (most of the time) and 20% the rest of the time ("white" periods: noon Friday through noon Saturday; 3 PM Sunday through noon Monday). On major holidays ("red" periods), there are no reductions. A calendar of red/white/blue periods is available at any station, and you can buy tickets at any station, too. Note that there is no reduction for buying a round-trip *(aller-retour)* ticket rather than a one-way *(aller simple)* ticket.

By Bus France's excellent train service means that long-distance buses are rare; regional buses, too, are found mainly where the train service is spotty. Excursions and bus holidays are organized by the SNCF and other tourist organizations, such as **Horizons Européens.** Ask for the brochure at any major travel agent, or contact **France-Tourisme** (3 rue d'Alger, 75001 Paris, tel. 42–61–85–50).

By Car Roads marked A *(Autoroutes)* are expressways. There are ex-
Road Conditions cellent links between Paris and most other French cities, but poor ones between the provinces (principal exception: the A9/A8 that runs the length of the Mediterranean). Most expressways require you to pay a toll *(péage);* the rates vary and can be steep. The N *(Route Nationale)* roads and D *(Route Départementale)* roads are usually wide, unencumbered, and fast (you can average 80 kph/50 mph with luck). The cheap, informative, and well-presented regional yellow Michelin maps are an invaluable navigational aid.

Rules of the Road You may use your home driver's license in France, but you must be able to prove that you have third-party insurance. Drive on the right. Be aware of the erratically followed French tradition of giving way to drivers coming from the right, unless there is an international stop sign. Seat belts are obligatory, and children under 12 may not travel in the front seat. Speed limits: 130 kph (81 mph) on expressways; 110 kph (68 mph) on major highways; 90 kph (56 mph) on minor rural roads; 50 kph (31 mph) in towns. French drivers break these limits and police dish out hefty on-the-spot fines with equal abandon.

Parking Parking is often difficult in large towns. Meters and ticket machines (pay and display) are commonplace (be sure to have a supply of 1-franc coins). In smaller towns, parking may be permitted on one side of the street only, alternating every two weeks: Pay attention to signs. The French park as anarchically as they drive, but don't follow their example: If you're caught out of bounds, you could be due for a hefty fine and your vehicle may be unceremoniously towed away to the dread compound (500 francs to retrieve it).

Gas Gas is more expensive on expressways and in rural areas. Don't let your tank get too low (if you're unlucky, you can go for many miles in the country without hitting a gas station) and keep an eye on pump prices as you go. These vary enormously: anything between 5 and 6 francs/liter. At the pumps, opt for "super" (high-grade/four-star) rather than "essence" (low-grade/two-star).

Breakdowns If you break down on an expressway, go to the nearest roadside emergency telephone and call the breakdown service. If you break down anywhere else, find the nearest garage or, failing all else, contact the police (dial 17).

By Boat France has Europe's densest inland waterway system, and canal and river vacation trips are popular. You can take an all-inclusive organized cruise or simply rent a boat and plan your own leisurely route. Contact a travel agent for details or ask for a *"Tourisme Fluvial"* brochure in any French tourist office. Request further information from French national tourist offices.

By Bicycle There is no shortage of wide, empty roads and flat or rolling countryside in France suitable for biking. The French themselves are great bicycling enthusiasts. Bikes can be hired from many train stations (ask for a list at any station) for around 40 francs a day; you need to show your passport and leave a deposit of 500 francs (unless you have Visa or Mastercard). In general, you must return the bike to a station within the same *département* (county or region). Bikes may be sent as accompanied luggage from any station in France; some trains in rural areas transport them without any extra charge.

Telephones

Local Calls The French telephone system is modern and efficient. Telephone booths are plentiful; they can almost always be found at post offices and often in cafés. A local call costs 73 centimes for the first minute plus 12 centimes per additional minute; half-price rates apply weekdays between 9:30 PM and 8 AM, from 1:30 PM Saturday, and all day Sunday.

Pay phones work principally with 50-centime, 1- and 5-franc coins (1 franc minimum). Lift the receiver, place the coin or coins in the appropriate slots, and dial. Unused coins are returned when you hang up. A vast number of French pay phones are now operated by cards *(télécartes)*, which you can buy from post offices and some tobacco shops, or *tabacs* (cost: 40 francs for 50 units; 96 francs for 120).

All French phone numbers have eight digits; a code is required only when calling the Paris region from the provinces (add 16–1 for Paris) and for calling the provinces from Paris (16 then the number). The number system was changed only in 1985; therefore, you may still come across some seven-digit numbers (in Paris) and some six-digit ones (elsewhere). Add 4 to the beginning of such Paris numbers, and the former two-figure area code to provincial ones.

International Calls Dial 19 and wait for the tone, then dial the country code (1 for the United States and Canada; 44 for the United Kingdom), area code (minus any initial 0), and number. Approximate daytime rate, per minute: 7.70 francs for the United States and Canada; 4.50 francs for the United Kingdom. Reduced rates, per minute: United States and Canada, 5.60 francs (2–noon daily) or 6.30 francs (noon–2 PM and 8 PM–2 AM weekdays, noon–2 AM Sunday); United Kingdom, 3 francs (9:30 PM–8 AM/2 AM–8 PM Saturday/all-day Sunday and holidays). AT&T's USA Direct program allows callers to take advantage of AT&T directly with the AT&T system. To do so from France dial 0011. You can then either dial direct (1 + area code + number), billing the call to a credit card, or make a collect call. For calls from outside the country, France's international telephone code number is 33.

Operators and Information To find a number in France or to request other information, dial 12. For international inquiries, dial 19–33 plus the country code.

Mail

Postal Rates Airmail letters to the United States and Canada cost 4 francs for 20 grams, 6.90 francs for 30 grams, 7.20 francs for 40 grams, and 7.50 francs for 50 grams. Letters to the United Kingdom cost 2.50 francs for up to 20 grams. Letters cost 2.50 francs within France; postcards cost 2.30 francs within France and if sent to Canada, the United States, the United Kingdom, and Common Market countries; 3.70 francs if sent airmail to North America. Stamps can be bought in post offices and cafés sporting a red TABAC sign outside.

Receiving Mail If you're uncertain where you'll be staying, have mail sent to **American Express** (tel. 800/543–4080 for a list of foreign offices) or to the local post office, addressed as **Poste Restante.** American Express has a $2 service charge per letter.

Tipping

The French have a clear idea of when they should be tipped. Bills in bars and restaurants include service, but it is customary to leave some small change unless you're dissatisfied. The amount of this varies: 30 centimes if you've merely bought a beer or a few francs after a meal. Tip taxi drivers and hairdressers about 10%. Give ushers in theaters and movie theaters 1 or 2 francs. In some theaters and hotels, coat check attendants may expect nothing (if there is a sign saying *Pourboire Interdit*— Tips Forbidden); otherwise give them 5 francs. Washroom attendants usually get 5 francs, though the sum is often posted.

If you stay in a hotel for more than two or three days, it is customary to leave something for the chambermaid—about 10 francs per day. In expensive hotels you may well call on the services of a baggage porter (bell boy) and hotel porter and possibly the telephone receptionist. All expect a tip: Plan on about 10 francs per item for the baggage boy, but the other tips will depend on how much you've used their services—common sense must guide you here. In hotels that provide room service, give 5 francs to the waiter (this does not apply to breakfast served in your room). If the chambermaid does some pressing or laundering for you, give her 5 francs on top of the charge made.

Gas-station attendants get nothing for gas or oil, and 5 or 10 francs for checking tires. Train and airport porters get a fixed sum (6–10 francs) per bag, but you're better off getting your own baggage cart if you can (a 10-franc coin—refundable—is sometimes necessary). Museum guides should get 5–10 francs after a guided tour, and it is standard practice to tip tour guides (and bus drivers) 10 francs or more after an excursion, depending on its length.

Opening and Closing Times

Banks Banks are open weekdays but have no strict pattern regarding times. In general, though, hours are from 9:30 to 4:30. Most banks, but not all, take a one-hour, or even a 90-minute, lunch break.

Museums Most museums are closed one day a week (usually Tuesday) and on national holidays. Usual opening times are from 9:30 to 5 or 6. Many museums close for lunch (noon–2); many are open afternoons only on Sunday.

Shops Large stores in big towns are open from 9 or 9:30 until 6 or 7 (without a lunch break). Smaller shops often open earlier (8 AM) and close later (8 PM) but take a lengthy lunch break (1–4). This siesta-type schedule is routine in the south of France. Corner groceries, often run by immigrants ("*l'Arabe du coin*"), frequently stay open until around 10 PM.

Shopping

VAT Refunds A number of shops, particularly large stores and shops in holiday resorts, offer VAT refunds to foreign shoppers. You are entitled to an Export Discount of 20%–30%, depending on the item purchased, but it is often applicable only if your purchases in the same store reach a minimum of 2,800 francs (for U.K. and Common Market residents) or 1,200 francs (other residents, including U.S. and Canadian).

Bargaining Shop prices are clearly marked and bargaining isn't a way of life. Still, at outdoor and flea markets and in antiques stores, you can try your luck. If you're thinking of buying several items, you've nothing to lose by cheerfully suggesting to the storeholder, "*Vous me faites un prix?*" ("How about a discount?").

Sports and Fitness

France has no shortage of sports facilities. Many seaside resorts are well equipped for **water sports,** such as windsurfing and waterskiing, and there are swimming pools in every French town.

Biking (*see* By Bicycle in Getting Around Provence and the Riviera, *above*) is a popular pastime and, like horseback riding (*equitation*), possible in many rural areas. Many rivers offer excellent **fishing** (check locally for authorization rights), and **canoeing** is good as well. **Tennis** is phenomenally popular, and courts are everywhere: Try for a typical *terre battue* (clay) court if you can. **Golf** and **squash** are common along the coast; you may be able to find a course or a court nearby. The French are not so keen on **jogging,** but you'll have no difficulty locating a suitable local park or avenue.

The sport that is closest to French hearts is ***boules*** or ***pétanque***—an easy-to-grasp version of bowling, traditionally played beneath plane trees with a glass of *pastis* (similar to anisette) at hand. The local *boulodrome* is a social focal point in southern France.

Beaches

It is ironic that France's most famous coastline should possess the country's worst beaches. But there it is: Sand is in shorter supply along the Riviera than pebbles. There are sandy beaches, of course, but they are seldom large or particularly clean, as the Mediterranean behaves like a large lake, with minimal tide to wash away the litter.

Dining

Eating in France is serious business. This is two-big-meals-a-day country, with good restaurants around every corner. If you prefer to eat lighter, you can try a *brasserie* for rapid, straightforward fare (steak and french fries remains the classic), a picnic (a *baguette* loaf with ham, cheese, or pâté makes a perfect combination), or one of the fast-food joints that have mushroomed in cities and towns over recent years. Snack possibilities—from pastry shops (*patisseries*) to pancake/roast chestnut street sellers—are legion.

French breakfasts are relatively skimpy: good coffee, fruit juice if you request it, bread, butter, and croissants. You can "breakfast" in cafés as well as hotels. If you're in the mood for bacon and eggs, however, you're in trouble.

Mealtimes Dinner is the main meal and usually begins at 8 PM. Lunch—starting at 12:30 or 1—can be as copious as you care to make it.

Precautions Tap water is safe, though not always appetizing. Mineral water—there is a vast choice of both still (*eau plate*) and fizzy (*eau gazeuse*)—is a palatable alternative. Perhaps the biggest eating problem in France is saying no: If you're invited to a French family's home, you will be encouraged, if not expected, to take two or three servings of everything offered.

Ratings Highly recommended restaurants are indicated by a star ★.

Category	Cost*: Major City	Cost*: Other Areas
Very Expensive	over 500 francs	over 400 francs
Expensive	250–500 francs	200–400 francs

Moderate	150–250 francs	100–200 francs
Inexpensive	under 150 francs	under 100 francs

per person for a three-course meal, including tax (18.6%) and tip but not wine

Lodging

Provence and the Riviera have a wide range of accommodations, ranging from rambling old village inns that cost next to nothing to stylish converted châteaus that cost the earth. Prices must, by law, be posted at the hotel entrance and should include taxes and service. Prices are always by room, not per person (ask for a *grand lit* if you want a double bed). Breakfast is not always included in this price, but you are usually expected to have it and are often charged for it regardless. In smaller rural hotels you may be expected to have your evening meal at the hotel, too.

Hotels Hotels are officially classified from one-star up to four-star/deluxe. France is not dominated by big hotel chains; examples in the upper price bracket include **Frantel, Holiday Inn, Novotel,** and **Sofitel.** The **Ibis** and **Climat de France** chains are more moderately priced; the new **Formula 1** chain provides basic comfort for up to three persons per room for 135 francs a night. Chain hotels, as a rule, lack atmosphere, with the following exceptions: **Logis de France** has small, inexpensive hotels that can be relied on for minimum standards of comfort, character, and regional cuisine. Watch for the distinctive yellow-and-green signs. The Logis de France paperback guide is widely available in bookshops (cost: around 65 francs) or from Logis de France (83 av. d'Italie, 75013 Paris). **France-Accueil** is another friendly, low-cost chain (free booklet from France-Accueil, 85 rue Dessous-des-Berges, 75013 Paris). You can stay in style at any of the prestigious **Relais & Châteaux** chain of converted chateaus and manor houses. Each hotel is distinctively furnished, provides top cuisine, and often stands in spacious grounds. A booklet listing members is available in bookshops or from Relais & Châteaux (9 av. Marceau, 75016 Paris).

Self-catering Best bets are the **Gîtes Ruraux,** which offer a family or group the possibility of a low-cost, self-catering vacation in a furnished cottage, chalet, or apartment in the country; rentals are by the week or month. For details contact either the **Maison des Gîtes de France** (35 rue Godot-de-Mauroy, 75009 Paris, tel. 47–42–20–20), naming which region interests you, or the **French Government Tourist Office** in London (178 Piccadilly, W1V OAL, tel. 01/491–7622), which runs a special reservation service.

Bed and Breakfast Bed-and-breakfasts, known in France as *Chambres d'Hôte*, are becoming increasingly popular, especially in rural areas. Check local tourist offices for details.

Youth Hostels Given that cheap hotel accommodations in France are so easy to find, there is scarcely any economic reason for staying in a youth hostel, especially since standards in France don't measure up to those in neighboring countries. If you enjoy a hostel ambience, however, you may care to note the address of the French headquarters (**Fédération Unie des Auberges de Jeunesse,** 10 rue Notre-Dame-de-Lorette, 75009 Paris).

Villas The French Government Tourist Offices in New York and London publish extensive lists of agencies specializing in villa rentals. You may also write to **Rent-a-Villa Ltd.** (3 W. 51st St., New York, NY 10019) or, in France, **Interhome** (15 av. Jean-Aicard, 75011 Paris).

Camping French campsites have a high reputation for organization and amenities, but they tend to be jam-packed in July and August. More and more campsites now welcome advance reservations; if you're traveling in summer, it makes good sense to book ahead. A guide to the country's campsites is published by the **Fédération Française de Camping et de Caravaning** (78 rue de Rivoli, 75004 Paris).

Ratings Highly recommended hotels are indicated by a star ★.

Category	Cost*: Major City	Cost*: Other Areas
Very Expensive	over 1,000 francs	over 800 francs
Expensive	600–1,000 francs	400–800 francs
Moderate	300–600 francs	200–400 francs
Inexpensive	under 300 francs	under 200 francs

All prices are for a standard double room for two, including tax (18.6%) and service charge.

Credit Cards

The following credit card abbreviations are used: AE, American Express; DC, Diners Club; MC, MasterCard; and V, Visa.

2 Portraits of Provence & the Riviera

Provence and the Riviera at a Glance: A Chronology

c 600 BC	Greek colonists found Marseille
after 500 BC	Celts appear in France
58–51 BC	Julius Caesar conquers Gaul; writes up the war in *De Bello Gallico*
52 BC	Lutetia, later to become Paris, is built by the Gallo-Romans
46 BC	Roman amphitheater built at Arles
14 BC	The Pont du Gard, the aqueduct at Nîmes, is erected
AD 212	Roman citizenship conferred on all free inhabitants of Gaul
406	Invasion by the Vandals (Germanic tribes)

The Merovingian Dynasty

486–511	Clovis, king of the Franks (481–511), defeats the Roman governor of Gaul and founds the Merovingian Dynasty. Great monasteries, such as those at Tours, Limoges, and Chartres, become centers of culture
732	Arab expansion checked at the Battles of Poitiers and Tours by Charles Martel

The Carolingian Dynasty

768–778	Charlemagne (768–814) becomes king of the Franks (768) and conquers northern Italy (774)
800	The pope crowns Charlemagne Holy Roman Emperor in Rome
814–987	Death of Charlemagne. The Carolingian line continues until 987 through a dozen or so monarchs, with a batch called Charles (the Bald, the Fat, the Simple) and a sprinkling of Louis. Under the Treaty of Verdun (843), the empire is divided in two—the eastern half becoming Germany, the western half France; Provence is given to Lothair I. Kingdom of Provence founded 879; joined to Arles in 933

The Capetian Dynasty

987	Hugh Capet (987–996) is elected king of France and establishes the principle of hereditary rule for his descendants
1112–1245	Provence ruled by counts of Barcelona
c 1150	Struggle between the Anglo-Norman kings (Angevin Empire) and the French; when Eleanor of Aquitaine switches husbands (from Louis VII of France to Henry II of England), her extensive lands pass to English rule
1204	Fourth Crusade: Franks conquer Byzantium and found the Latin Empire
1245–1481	Provence ruled by dukes of Anjou

1270   Louis IX (1226–70), the only French king to achieve sainthood, dies in Tunis on the seventh and last Crusade

1302–07   Philippe IV (1285–1314), the Fair, calls together the first States-General, predecessor to the French Parliament. He disbands the Knights Templars to gain their wealth (1307)

1309   Papacy escapes from a corrupt and disorderly Rome to Avignon in southern France, where it stays for nearly 70 years

The Valois Dynasty

1337–1453   Hundred Years' War between France and England: episodic fighting for control of those areas of France gained by the English crown following the marriage of Eleanor of Aquitaine and Henry II

1348–1350   The Black Death rages in France

1453   France finally defeats England, terminating the Hundred Years' War and the English claim to the French throne

c 1490   Provence annexed to France

1494   Italian wars: beginning of Franco-Habsburg struggle for hegemony in Europe

1515–47   Reign of François I, who imports Italian artists, including Leonardo da Vinci (1452–1519), and brings the Renaissance to France

1562–98   Wars of Religion (Catholics versus Protestants/Huguenots) within France

The Bourbon Dynasty

1589   The first Bourbon king, Henry IV (1589–1610), is a Huguenot who converts to Catholicism and achieves peace in France. He signs the Edict of Nantes, giving limited freedom of worship to Protestants

1643–1715   Reign of Louis XIV, the Sun King, an absolute monarch who builds the Baroque power base of Versailles and presents Europe with a glorious view of France. With his first minister, Colbert, Louis makes France, by force of arms, the most powerful nation-state in Europe. He persecutes the Huguenots, who emigrate in great numbers, nearly ruining the French economy

1660   Classical period of French culture: writers Molière (1622–73), Jean Racine (1639–99), Pierre Corneille (1606–84), and painter Nicolas Poussin (1594–1665)

1700 onward   Writer and pedagogue Voltaire (1694–1778) is a central figure in the French Enlightenment, along with Jean-Jacques Rousseau (1712–78) and Denis Diderot (1713–84), who, in 1751, compiles the first modern encyclopedia. In the arts, painter Jacques Louis David (1748–1825) reinforces revolutionary creeds in his severe neoclassical works

1776   The French assist in the American War of Independence. Ideals of liberty cross the Atlantic with the returning troops to reinforce new social concepts

The French Revolution

1789–1804   The Bastille is stormed on July 14, 1789. Following upon early Republican ideals comes the Terror and the administration of the Directory under Robespierre. There are widespread political executions—Louis XVI and his queen, Marie Antoinette, are guillotined in 1793. Reaction sets in, and the instigators of the Terror are themselves executed (1794). Napoleon Bonaparte enters the scene as the champion of the Directory (1795–99) and is installed as First Consul during the Consulate (1799–1804)

1790   The departments of Bouches-du-Rhône, Var, and Basses-Alpes, and parts of Drôme, Alpes-Maritimes, and Vaucluse are formed from Provence.

The First Empire

1804   Napoleon crowns himself Emperor of France at Notre-Dame in the presence of the pope

1805–12   Napoleon conquers most of Europe. The Napoleonic Age is marked by a neoclassical style in the arts, called Empire, as well as by the rise of Romanticism

1812–14   Winter cold and Russian determination defeat Napoleon outside Moscow. The emperor abdicates and is transported to Elba in the Mediterranean (1814)

Restoration of the Bourbons

1814–15   Louis XVIII, brother of the executed Louis XVI, regains the throne after the Congress of Vienna is held to settle peace terms

1815   The Hundred Days: Napoleon returns from Elba and musters an army on his march to the capital, but lacks national support. He is defeated at Waterloo (June 18) and exiled to the island of St. Helena in the South Atlantic

1821   Napoleon dies in exile

1830   Bourbon king Charles X, locked into a prerevolutionary state of mind, abdicates. A brief upheaval (Three Glorious Days) brings Louis-Philippe, the Citizen King, to the throne

1846–48   Severe industrial and farming depression contributes to Louis-Philippe's abdication (1848)

Second Republic and Second Empire

1848–52   Louis-Napoleon (nephew and step-grandson of Napoleon I) is elected president of the short-lived Second Republic. He makes a successful attempt to assume supreme power and is declared emperor of France, taking the title Napoleon III

1863   Napoleon III inaugurates the Salon des Refusés in response to critical opinion. It includes work by Edouard Manet (1832–83), Claude Monet (1840–1926), and Paul Cézanne (1839–1906) and is commonly regarded as the birthplace of Impressionism and of modern art in general

The Third Republic

1874   Emergence of the Impressionist school of painting: Monet, Pierre Auguste Renoir (1841–1919), and Edgar Degas (1834–1917)

1914–18   During World War I, France fights with the Allies, opposing Germany, Austria-Hungary, and Turkey

1918–39   Between wars, France attracts artists and writers, including Americans—Ernest Hemingway (1899–1961) and Gertrude Stein (1874–1946). France nourishes major artistic movements: Constructivism, Dadaism, Surrealism, and Existentialism

1939–45   At the beginning of World War II, France fights with the Allies until invaded and defeated by Germany in 1940

1944–46   A provisional government takes power under General de Gaulle; American aid assists French recovery

The Fourth Republic

1946   France adopts a new constitution; French women gain the right to vote

1957   The Treaty of Rome establishes the European Economic Community (now known as the European Community—EC), with France a founding member

The Fifth Republic

1958–68   De Gaulle is the first president under a new constitution; he resigns in 1968 after widespread disturbances

1981   François Mitterrand is elected the first Socialist president of France since World War II

1988   Mitterrand is elected for a second term

1989   Bicentennial celebration of the French Revolution

1990   TGV train clocks a world record—515 kph (322 mph)—on a practice run. Channel Tunnel link-up between French and English workers

Postcards from Summer

By Peter Mayle

In his second popular book on life in Provence, Toujours Provence, *British writer Peter Mayle wittily evokes the charms and idiosyncracies of locals and visitors alike.*

It has taken us three years to accept the fact that we live in the same house, but in two different places.

What we think of as normal life starts in September. Apart from market days in the towns, there are no crowds. Traffic on the back roads is sparse during the day—a tractor, a few vans—and virtually nonexistent at night. There is always a table in every restaurant, except perhaps for Sunday lunch. Social life is intermittent and uncomplicated. The baker has bread, the plumber has time for a chat, the postman has time for a drink. After the first deafening weekend of the hunting season, the forest is quiet. Each field has a stooped, reflective figure working among the vines, very slowly up one line, very slowly down the next. The hours between noon and two are dead.

And then we come to July and August.

We used to treat them as just another two months of the year; hot months, certainly, but nothing that required much adjustment on our part except to make sure that the afternoon included a siesta.

We were wrong. Where we live in July and August is still the Lubéron, but it's not the same Lubéron. It is the Lubéron *en vacances*, and our past efforts to live normally during abnormal times have been miserably unsuccessful. So unsuccessful that we once considered cancelling summer altogether and going somewhere grey and cool and peaceful, like the Hebrides.

But if we did, we would probably miss it, all of it, even the days and incidents that have reduced us to sweating, irritated, overtired zombies. So we have decided to come to terms with the Lubéron in the summer, to do our best to join the rest of the world on holiday and, like them, to send postcards telling distant friends about the wonderful time we are having. Here are a few.

Saint-Tropez   *Cherchez les nudistes!* It is open season for nature lovers, and there is likely to be a sharp increase in the number of applicants wishing to join the Saint-Tropez police force.

The mayor, Monsieur Spada, has flown in the face of years of tradition (Saint-Tropez made public nudity famous, after all) and has decreed that in the name of safety and hygiene there will be no more naked sunbathing on the public beaches. *"Le nudisme intégral est interdit,"* says Monsieur Spada, and he has empowered the police to seize and arrest any offenders. Well, perhaps not to seize them, but to track them down and fine them 75 francs, or as much as 1,500 francs if they have been guilty of creating a public outrage.

Exactly where a nudist might keep 1,500 francs is a question that is puzzling local residents.

Meanwhile, a defiant group of nudists has set up headquarters in some rocks behind *la plage de la Moutte*. A spokeswoman for the group has said that under no circumstances would bathing suits be worn. Wish you were here.

The Melon Field Faustin's brother Jacky, a wiry little man of 60 or so, grows melons in the field opposite the house. It's a large field, but he does all the work himself, and by hand. In the spring I have often seen him out there for six or seven hours, back bent like a hinge, his hoe chopping at the weeds that threaten to strangle his crop. He doesn't spray—who would eat a melon tasting of chemicals?—and I think he must enjoy looking after his land in the traditional way.

Now that the melons are ripening, he comes to the field at 6 every morning to pick the ones that are ready. He takes them up to Ménerbes to be packed in shallow wooden crates. From Ménerbes they go to Cavaillon, and from Cavaillon to Avignon, to Paris, everywhere. It amuses Jacky to think of people in smart restaurants paying *une petite fortune* for a simple thing like a melon.

If I get up early enough I can catch him before he goes to Ménerbes. He always has a couple of melons that are too ripe to travel, and he sells them to me for a few francs.

As I walk back to the house, the sun clears the top of the mountain and it is suddenly hot on my face. The melons, heavy and satisfying in my hands, are still cool from the night air. We have them for breakfast, fresh and sweet, less than 10 minutes after they have been picked.

Behind the Bar There is a point at which a swimming pool ceases to be luxury and becomes very close to a necessity, and that point is when the temperature hits 100 degrees. Whenever people ask us about renting a house for the summer, we always tell them this, and some of them listen.

Others don't, and within two days of arriving they are on the phone telling us what we told them months before. It's so *hot*, they say. Too hot for tennis, too hot for cycling, too hot for sightseeing, too hot, too hot. Oh, for a pool. You're so lucky.

There is a hopeful pause. Is it my imagination, or can I actually hear the drops of perspiration falling like summer rain on the pages of the telephone directory?

I suppose the answer is to be callous but helpful. There is a public swimming pool near Apt, if you don't mind sharing the water with a few hundred small brown dervishes on their school holidays. There is the Mediterranean, only an hour's drive away; no, with traffic it could take two hours. Make sure you have some bottles of Evian in the car. It wouldn't do to get dehydrated.

Or you could close the shutters against the sun, spend the day in the house, and spring forth refreshed into the evening air. It would be difficult to acquire the souvenir suntan, but at least there would be no chance of heatstroke.

These brutal and unworthy suggestions barely have time to cross my mind before the voice of despair turns into the voice of relief. Of course! We could come over in the morning for a quick dip without disturbing you. Just a splash. You won't even know we've been.

They come at noon, with friends. They swim. They take the sun. Thirst creeps up on them, much to their surprise, and that's why I'm behind the bar. My wife is in the kitchen, making lunch for six. *Vivent les vacances*.

The Night Walk The dogs cope with the heat by sleeping through it, stretched out in the courtyard or curled in the shade of the rosemary hedge. They come to life as the pink in the sky is turning to darkness, sniffing the breeze, jostling each other around our feet in their anticipation of a walk. We take the flashlight and follow them into the forest.

It smells of warm pine needles and baked earth, dry and spicy when we step on a patch of thyme. Small, invisible creatures slither away from us and rustle through the leaves of the wild box that grows like a weed.

Sounds carry: *cigales* and frogs, the muffled thump of music through the open window of a faraway house, the clinks and murmurs of dinner drifting up from Faustin's terrace. The hills on the other side of the valley, uninhabited for 10 months a year, are pricked with lights that will be switched off at the end of August.

We get back to the house and take off our shoes, and the warmth of the flagstones is an invitation to swim. A dive into dark water, and then a last glass of wine. The sky is clear except for a jumble of stars; it will be hot again tomorrow. Hot and slow, just like today.

Knee-deep in Lavender I had been cutting lavender with a pair of pruning shears and I was making a slow, amateurish job of it, nearly an hour to do fewer than a dozen clumps. When Henriette arrived at the house with a basket of aubergines, I was pleased to have the chance to stop. Henriette looked at the lavender, looked at the pruning shears, and shook her head at the ignorance of her neighbor. Didn't I know how to cut lavender? What was I doing with those pruning shears? Where was my *faucille?*

She went to her van and came back with a blackened sickle, its needle-sharp tip embedded in an old wine cork for safety. It was surprisingly light, and felt sharp enough to shave with. I made a few passes with it in the air, and Henriette shook her head again. Obviously, I needed a lesson.

She hitched up her skirt and attacked the nearest row of lavender, gathering the long stems into a tight bunch with one arm and slicing them off at the bottom with a single smooth pull of the sickle. In five minutes she had cut more than I had in an hour. It looked easy; bend, gather, pull. Nothing to it.

"Voilà!" said Henriette. "When I was a little girl in the Basses-Alpes, we had hectares of lavender, and no machines. Everyone used the *faucille*."

She passed it back to me, told me to mind my legs, and went off to join Faustin in the vines.

It wasn't as easy as it looked, and my first effort produced a ragged, uneven clump, more chewed than sliced. I realized that the sickle was made for right-handed lavender cutters, and had to compensate for being left-handed by slicing away from me. My wife came out to tell me to mind my legs. She doesn't trust me with sharp implements, and so she was reassured to see me cutting away from the body. Even with my genius for self-inflicted wounds there seemed to be little risk of amputation.

I had just come to the final clump when Henriette came back. I looked up, hoping for praise, and sliced my index finger nearly through to the bone. There was a great deal of blood, and Henriette asked me if I was giving myself a manicure. I sometimes wonder about her sense of humor. Two days later she gave me a sickle of my very own, and told me that I was forbidden to use it unless I was wearing gloves.

The Alcoholic Tendencies of Wasps The Provençal wasp, although small, has an evil sting. He also has an ungallant, hit-and-run method of attack in the swimming pool. He paddles up behind his unsuspecting victim, waits until an arm is raised, and—*tok!*—strikes deep into the armpit. It hurts for several hours, and often causes people who have been stung to dress in protective clothing before they go swimming. This is the local version of the Miss Wet T-shirt contest.

I don't know whether all wasps like water, but here they love it—floating in the shallow end, dozing in the puddles on the flagstones, keeping an eye out for the unguarded armpit and the tender extremity—and after one disastrous day during which not only armpits but inner thighs received direct hits (obviously, some wasps can hold their breath and operate under water), I was sent off to look for wasp traps.

When I found them, in a *droguerie* in the back alleys of Cavaillon, I was lucky enough to find a wasp expert behind the counter. He demonstrated for me the latest model in traps, a plastic descendant of the old glass hanging traps that can sometimes be found in flea markets. It had been specially designed, he said, for use around swimming pools, and could be made irresistible to wasps.

It was in two parts. The base was a round bowl, raised off the ground by three flat supports, with a funnel leading up from the bottom. The top fitted over the lower bowl and prevented wasps who had made their way up the funnel from escaping.

But that, said the wasp expert, was the simple part. More difficult, more subtle, more artistic, was the bait. How does one persuade the wasp to abandon the pleasures of the flesh and climb up the funnel into the trap? What could tempt him away from the pool?

After spending some time in Provence, you learn to expect a brief lecture with every purchase, from an organically grown cabbage (two minutes) to a bed (half an hour or more, depending on the state of your back). For wasp traps, you should allow between 10 and 15 minutes. I sat on the stool in front of the counter and listened.

Wasps, it turned out, like alcohol. Some wasps like it *sucré*, others like it fruity, and there are even those who will crawl anywhere for a drop of *anis*. It is, said the expert, a matter of experimentation, a balancing of flavors and consistencies until one finds the blend that suits the palate of the local wasp population.

He suggested a few basic recipes: sweet vermouth with honey and water, diluted *crème de cassis*, dark beer spiked with *marc*, neat *pastis*. As an added inducement, the funnel can be lightly coated with honey, and a small puddle of water should always be left immediately beneath the funnel.

The expert set up a trap on the counter, and with two fingers imitated a wasp out for a stroll.

He stops, attracted by the puddle of water. The fingers stopped. He approaches the water, and then he becomes aware of something delicious above him. He climbs up the funnel to investigate, he jumps into his cocktail, *et voilà!*— he is unable to get out, being too drunk to crawl back down the funnel. He dies, but he dies happy.

I bought two traps, and tried out the recipes. All of them worked, which leads me to believe that the wasp has a serious drinking problem. And now, if ever a guest is overcome by strong waters, he is described as being as pissed as a wasp.

Maladie du Lubéron Most of the seasonal ailments of summer, while they may be uncomfortable or painful or merely embarrassing, are at least regarded with some sympathy. A man convalescing after an explosive encounter with one *merguez* sausage too many is not expected to venture back into polite society until his constitution has recovered. The same is true of third-degree sunburn, *rosé* poisoning, scorpion bites, a surfeit of garlic, or the giddiness and nausea caused by prolonged exposure to French bureaucracy. One suffers, but one is allowed to suffer alone and in peace.

There is another affliction, worse than scorpions or rogue sausages, which we have experienced ourselves and seen many times in other permanent residents of this quiet corner of France. Symptoms usually appear some time around mid-July and persist until early September: glazed and bloodshot eyes, yawning, loss of appetite, shortness of temper, lethargy, and a mild form of paranoia that manifests itself in sudden urges to join a monastery.

This is the *maladie du Lubéron,* or creeping social fatigue, and it provokes about the same degree of sympathy as a millionaire's servant problems.

If we examine the patients—the permanent residents—we can see why it happens. Permanent residents have their work, their local friends, their unhurried routines. They made a deliberate choice to live in the Lubéron instead of one of the cocktail capitals of the world because they wanted, if not to get away from it all, to get away from most of it. This eccentricity is understood and tolerated for 10 months a year.

Try to explain that in July and August. Here come the visitors, fresh from the plane or hot off the *autoroute,* panting for social action. Let's meet some of the locals! To hell with the book in the hammock and the walk in the woods. To hell with solitude; they want people—people for lunch, people for drinks, people for dinner—and so invitations and counterinvitations fly back and forth until every day for weeks has its own social highlight.

As the holiday comes to an end with one final multibottle dinner, it is possible to see even on the visitors' faces some traces of weariness. They had no idea it was so lively down here. They are only half-joking when they say they're going to need a rest to get over the whirl of the past few days. Is it always like this? How do you keep it up?

It isn't, and we don't. Like many of our friends, we collapse in between visitations, guarding empty days and free evenings, eating little and drinking less, going to bed early. And every year, when the dust has settled, we talk to other members of the distressed residents' association about ways of making summer less of an endurance test.

We all agree that firmness is the answer. Say no more often than yes. Harden the heart against the surprise visitor who cannot find a hotel room, the deprived child who has no swimming pool, the desperate traveler who has lost his wallet. Be firm; be helpful, be kind, be rude, but above all *be firm.*

And yet I know—I think we all know—that next summer will be the same. I suppose we must enjoy it. Or we would, if we weren't exhausted.

Place du Village   Cars have been banned from the village square, and stalls or trestle tables have been set up on three sides. On the fourth, a framework of scaffolding, blinking with colored lights, supports a raised platform made from wooden planks. Outside the café, the usual single row of tables and chairs has been multiplied by 10, and an extra waiter has been taken on to serve the sprawl of customers stretching from the butcher's down to the post office. Children and dogs chase each other through the crowd, stealing lumps of sugar from the tables and dodging the old men's sticks that are waved in mock anger. Nobody will go to bed early tonight, not even the children, because this is the village's annual party, the *fête votive*.

It begins in the late afternoon with a *pot d'amitié* in the square and the official opening of the stalls. Local artisans, the men's faces shining from an afternoon shave, stand behind their tables, glass in hand, or make final adjustments to their displays. There is pottery and jewelry, honey and lavender essence, hand-woven fabrics, iron and stone artifacts, paintings and wood carvings, books, postcards, tooled leatherwork, corkscrews with twisted olive-wood handles, patterned sachets of dried herbs. The woman selling pizza does brisk business as the first glass of wine begins to make the crowd hungry.

People drift off, eat, drift back. The night comes down, warm and still, the mountains in the distance just visible as deep black humps against the sky. The three-man accordion band tunes up on the platform and launches into the first of many *paso dobles* while the rock group from Avignon that will follow later rehearses on beer and *pastis* in the café.

The first dancers appear—an old man and his granddaughter, her nose pressed into his belt buckle, her feet balanced precariously on his feet. They are joined by a mother, father, and daughter dancing *à trois*, and then by several elderly couples, holding each other with stiff formality, their faces set with concentration as they try to retrace the steps they learned 50 years ago.

The *paso doble* session comes to an end with a flourish and a ruffle of accordions and drums, and the rock group warms up with five minutes of electronic tweaks that bounce off the old stone walls of the church opposite the platform.

The group's singer, a well-built young lady in tight black Lycra and a screaming orange wig, has attracted an audience before singing a note. An old man, the peak of his cap almost meeting the jut of his chin, has dragged a chair across from the café to sit directly in front of the microphone. As the singer starts her first number, some village boys made bold by his example come out of the shadows to stand by the old man's chair. All of them stare as though hypnotized at the shiny black pelvis rotating just above their heads.

The village girls, short of partners, dance with each other, as close as possible to the backs of the mesmerized boys. One of the waiters puts down his tray to caper in front of a pretty girl sitting with her parents. She blushes and ducks her head, but her mother nudges her to dance. Go on. The holiday will soon be over.

After an hour of music that threatens to dislodge the windows of the houses around the square, the group performs its finale. With an intensity worthy of Piaf on a sad night, the singer gives us *"Comme d'habitude,"* or "My Way," ending with a sob, her orange head bent over the microphone. The old man nods and bangs his stick on the ground, and the dancers go back to the café to see if there's any beer left.

Normally, there would have been *feux d'artifice* shooting up from the field behind the war memorial. This year, because of the drought, fireworks are forbidden. But it was a good *fête*. And did you see how the postman danced?

3 Provence

As you approach Provence, there is a magical moment when the north is finally left behind: Cypresses and red-tiled roofs appear; you hear the screech of the cicadas and catch the scent of wild thyme and lavender. Even on the modern highway, oleanders flower on the central strip against a backdrop of harsh, brightly lit landscapes that inspired the paintings of Paul Cézanne and Vincent Van Gogh.

Provence lies in the south of France, bordered by Italy to the east and the blue waters of the Mediterranean. The Romans called it Provincia—The Province—for it was the first part of Gaul they occupied. Roman remains litter the ground in well-preserved profusion. The theater and triumphal arch at Orange, the amphitheater at Nîmes, the aqueduct at Pont-du-Gard, and the mausoleum at St-Rémy-de-Provence are considered the best of their kind in existence.

Provençal life continues at an old-fashioned pace. Hot afternoons tend to mean siestas, with signs of life discernible only as the shadows under the *platanes* (plane trees) start to lengthen and lethargic locals saunter out to play *boules* (the French version of bocce) and drink long, cooling *pastis*, an anise-based aperitif.

Provence means dazzling light and rugged, rocky countryside, interspersed with vineyards, fields of lavender, and olive groves. Any Provençal market provides a glimpse of the bewildering variety of olives and herbs cultivated, and the local cuisine is pungently spiced with thyme, rosemary, basil, and garlic.

The famous *mistral*—a fierce, cold wind that races through the Rhône Valley—is another feature of Provence. It's claimed that the extensive network of expressways has lessened the mistral's effect, but you may have trouble believing this as the wind whistles around your ears. Thankfully, clear blue skies usually follow in its wake.

The Rhône, the great river of southern France, splits in two at Arles, 15 miles before reaching the Mediterranean: The Petit Rhône crosses the region known as the Camargue on its way to Saintes-Maries-de-la-Mer, while the Grand Rhône heads off to Fos, an industrial port just along the coast from Marseille.

A number of towns have grown up along the Rhône Valley owing to its historical importance as a communications artery. The biggest is dowdy, bustling Marseille; Orange, Avignon, Tarascon, and Arles have more picturesque charm. The Camargue, on the other hand, is the realm of birds and beasts; pink flamingoes and wild horses feel more at home among its marshy wastes than people ever could.

North of Marseille lies Aix-en-Provence, whose old-time elegance reflects its former role as regional capital. We have extended Provence's traditional boundaries westward slightly into Languedoc, to include historic Nîmes and the dynamic university town of Montpellier. The Riviera, meanwhile, is part of Provence—but so full of interest that we devote an entire chapter to it.

Essential Information

Important Addresses and Numbers

Tourist Information
Provence's two regional tourist offices accept written inquiries only. **Comité Régional du Tourisme du Languedoc-Roussillon** (27 rue Aiguillerie, 34000 Montpellier, tel. 67–22–81–00) will provide information on all towns west of the River Rhône, while the remainder of towns covered in this chapter are handled by the **Comité Régional du Tourisme de Provence-Alpes–Côte d'Azur** (Immeuble C.M.C.E., 2 rue Henri-Barbusse, 13241 Marseille, tel. 91–39–38–00).

Local tourist offices for major towns covered in this chapter are as follows: **Aix-en-Provence** (2 pl. du Général-de-Gaulle, tel. 42–26–02–93), **Arles** (35 pl. de la République, tel. 90–93–49–11), **Avignon** (41 cours Jean-Jaurès, tel. 90–82–65–11), **Marseille** (4 La Canebière, tel. 91–54–91–11), **Montpellier** (Pl. René-Devic, tel. 67–58–67–58), **Nîmes** (6 rue Auguste, tel. 66–67–29–11), and **Toulon** (8 av. Colbert, tel. 94–22–08–22).

Travel Agencies
Wagons-Lits (10 rue Portail-Boquier, Avignon, tel. 90–82–20–56; 67 La Canebière, Marseille, tel. 91–90–12–46; Midi-Libre Voyages, 20 blvd. de l'Amiral-Courbet, Nîmes, tel. 66–67–45–34; 3 rue des Cordeliers, Aix-en-Provence, tel. 42–96–31–88).

Car Rental
Avis (11 cours Gambetta, Aix-en-Provence, tel. 42–21–64–16; 267 blvd. National, Marseille, tel. 91–50–70–11; and 92 blvd. Rabatau, Marseille, tel. 91–80–12–00), **Europcar** (2 bis av. Victor-Hugo, Arles, tel. 90–93–23–24; 29 av. St-Ruf, Avignon, tel. 90–82–49–85), and **Hertz** (Parking des Gares, 18 rue Jules-Ferry, Montpellier, tel. 67–58–65–18; 5 blvd. de Prague, Nîmes, tel. 66–76–25–91).

Arriving and Departing

By Plane
The airports at Marseille and Montpellier are served by frequent flights from Paris and London, and there are daily flights from Paris to the smaller airport at Nîmes. Nice (*see* Chapter 4) is only 160 kilometers (100 miles) from Aix-en-Provence, and there are direct flights from the United States. If you plan to rent a car on arrival, the airports of Marseille and Montpellier are equally easy to leave without driving into either town.

By Car
The A6/A7 expressway (toll road) from Paris is known as the Autoroute du Soleil—the Expressway of the Sun—and takes you straight to Provence, whereupon it divides at Orange.

By Train
Avignon is fewer than four hours from Paris by high-speed train (TGV); trains depart from Paris's Gare de Lyon station.

Getting Around

By Car
After the A7 divides at Orange, the A9 heads west to Nîmes and Montpellier (765 kilometers/475 miles from Paris), extending into the Pyrénées and across the Spanish border. A7 continues southeast from Orange to Marseille on the coast (1,100 kilometers/680 miles from Paris), while A8 goes to Aix-en-Provence, and then to the Riviera and Italy.

By Train
After the main line divides at Avignon, the westbound link heads to Nîmes, Montpellier (fewer than five hours from Paris

by TGV), and points west. The southeast-bound link takes in Marseille (also fewer than five hours from Paris by TGV), Toulon, and the Riviera.

By Bus A moderately good network of bus services links places not served, or badly served, by the railway. If you plan to explore Provence by bus, Avignon is the best base. The town is well served by local buses, and excursion buses and boat trips down the Rhône start from here.

Guided Tours

The regional tourist offices' "52 Week" program pools 52 tours offered by various agencies, allowing visitors to choose from a myriad of tours throughout the year, touching on wine tasting, sailing, hang gliding, golfing, gastronomy, and cultural exploration. Contact **Loisirs-Acceuil** (Domaine de Vergon, 13370 Mallemort, tel. 90–59–18–05) for details. In addition, local tourist offices can arrange many tours, ranging from one-hour guided walks to excursions that take a week or longer by bus, by bicycle, on horseback, or on foot.

Bus Tours The **Comité Départemental du Tourisme** (6 rue. Jeune-Anacharsis, 13006 Marseille, tel. 91–54–92–66) offers a five-day bus tour called "Découverte de la Provence," which includes full board in two-star hotels and entry to all places of interest. The tour starts in Marseille, continues to Cassis (from which there is a boat trip in the fjordlike waterways known as *calanques*), and includes a day in the Camargue and visits to Aix-en-Provence, Les Baux, and Arles; the cost is 1,900 francs per person. **Capodano Voyages** (110 blvd. des Dames, 13002 Marseille, tel. 91–91–10–91) offers a "Bouillabaisse Weekend" in Marseille, taking in a trip to the harbor, the Château d'If, and Les Iles de Frioul; the cost is 2,750 francs per person. The **Arles Tourist Office** (35 pl. de la République, tel. 90–93–49–11) employs 15 guide-lecturers to run excursions of the town and region.

Horseback Tours The **Office Municipal de Tourisme** in Marseille features a six-day guided tour on horseback, during which you can stay in simple houses or tents. Beginning near Marseille in the hills of the Massif de la Sainte-Beaune, the tour continues through some wild but picturesque countryside, including Cézanne's mountain, La Sainte-Victoire; the cost, including insurance, is 2,750 francs per person. Twenty-seven kilometers (17 miles) from Aix-en-Provence lies **Ranch Lou Maze** (13680 Lançon de Provence, tel. 90–57–74–17), which offers horseback excursions of the Camargue; the cost ranges from 250 to 400 francs a day.

Special-Interest Tours **Capodano Voyages** (*see* Bus Tours, *above*) offers a two-day "Wines of the Sun and Gastronomy" tour that includes Avignon, a trip to the "Wine University" at Suze-la-Rousse, and stops at Orange and Villeneuve-les-Avignon. The price for one person is 1,300 francs, though it is lower for groups of two or more.

Exploring Provence

Numbers in the margin correspond to points of interest on the Provence and Nîmes maps.

Orientation

We have divided Provence into three exploring tours, each follows directly from the other. The marshy Camargue forms the heart of our first tour, which ventures briefly into the Languedoc region to visit the fine old towns of Nîmes and Montpellier before wheeling back across the Camargue to examine the Roman remains at Arles and St-Rémy. The tour finishes at Tarascon on the Rhône. The second tour begins farther up the river valley at Avignon, with its papal palace. This tour falls neatly within the boundaries of the Vaucluse *département*, ranging from Avignon in the south to the Roman towns of Orange and Vaison-la-Romaine to the north; the main natural feature is Mont Ventoux, towering above surrounding plains. The third tour begins in Aix, the historic capital of Provence, then heads south to Marseille and east along the spectacular Mediterranean coast to Toulon.

Highlights for First-time Visitors

Aix-en-Provence, Tour 3
Roman remains at Arles, Tour 1
Palais des Papes (Papal palace), Avignon, Tour 2
Roman remains at Nîmes, Tour 1
Pont du Gard, Tour 1
St-Remy-de-Provence, Tour 1
Théâtre Antique, Orange, Tour 2
Les Baux-de-Provence, Tour 1

Tour 1: Nîmes and the Camargue

The first tour starts with a bridge, symbolically linking the 20th century to the Roman grandeur that haunts Provence: the **❶ Pont du Gard**, midway between Avignon and Nîmes off the N86 highway (take D981 at Remoulins; if you arrive by the A9 expressway, take the Remoulins exit).

The Pont du Gard is a huge, three-tiered aqueduct, erected 2,000 years ago as part of a 30-mile canal supplying water to Roman Nîmes. It is astonishingly well preserved. Its setting, spanning a rocky gorge 150 feet above the River Gardon, is nothing less than spectacular. There is no entry fee or guide, and at certain times you can have it all to yourself: Early morning is best, when the honey-colored stone gleams in the sunlight. The best way to gauge the full majesty of the Pont du Gard is to walk right along the top.

Time Out In the enchanting little medieval town of Uzès, 14 kilometers (9 miles) northwest via D981, the **Alexandry** restaurant is a good choice for an inexpensive bite to eat. *6 blvd. Gambetta.*

❷ Nîmes lies 20 kilometers (13 miles) southwest of the Pont du Gard (via N86) and 24 kilometers (15 miles) south of Uzès (via D979). Few towns have preserved such visible links with their Roman past: Nemausus, as the town was then known, grew to prominence during the reign of Caesar Augustus (27 BC–AD 14) and still boasts a Roman amphitheater (Arènes), temple (Maison Carrée), and watchtower (Tour Magne). Luckily, these monuments emerged relatively unscathed from the cataclysmic

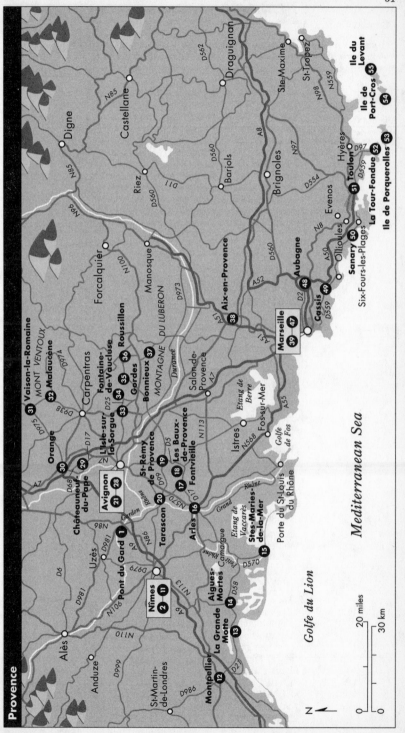

Provence

Mediterranean Sea

Golfe du Lion

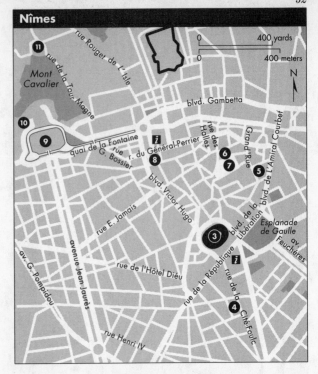

flash-flood that devastated Nîmes in 1988, leaving thousands homeless.

3 Start out at place des Arènes, site of the **Arènes**, a smaller version of the Colosseum in Rome and considered to be the world's best-preserved Roman amphitheater, which is over 140 yards long and 110 yards wide, with a seating capacity of 21,000. Despite its checkered history—it was transformed into a fortress by the Visigoths and used for housing in medieval times—the arena has been restored to most of its original splendor. An inflatable roof covers the amphitheater during the winter, when various exhibits and expositions occupy the space. Bullfights and tennis tournaments are held here in summer. *Blvd. Victor-Hugo, tel. 66-76-72-77. Admission: 20 frs. adults, children under 10 free; joint ticket to Arènes and Tour Magne: 28 frs. adults, 17 frs. children. Open mid-June–mid-Sept., daily 8–8; mid-Sept.–Oct. and Apr.–mid-June, daily 9–noon and 2–6; Nov.–Mar., daily 9–noon and 2–5.*

4 Take rue de la Cité-Foulc behind the Arènes to the **Musée des Beaux-Arts** (Fine Arts Museum), where you can admire a vast Roman mosaic discovered in Nîmes during the past century; the marriage ceremony depicted in the center of the mosaic provides intriguing insights into the Roman aristocratic lifestyle. Old Masters (Nicolas Poussin, Pieter Brueghel, Peter Paul Rubens) and sculpture (Auguste Rodin and his pupil Émile Bourdelle) form the mainstay of the collection. *Rue de la Cité-Foulc, tel. 66-67-32-08. Admission: 15 frs. adults, 10 frs. children. Open Tues.–Sat. 9:30–12:30 and 2–6, Sun. and Mon. 2–6.*

Return to the Arènes and head right, along boulevard de la Libération, which soon becomes boulevard de l'Amiral-Courbet.
⑤ A hundred and fifty yards down on the left is the **Musée Archéologique et d'Histoire Naturelle,** rich in local archaeological finds, mainly statues, busts, friezes, tools, glass, and pottery. It also houses an extensive collection of Greek, Roman, and medieval coins. *Blvd. de l'Amiral-Courbet, tel. 66–67–25–57. Admission free. Open Tues.–Sat. 9:30–12:30 and 2–6, Sun. and Mon. 1:30–6.*

Turn right into Grand' Rue behind the museum, then take the
⑥ second left up toward the **cathedral.** This uninspired 19th-century reconstruction is of less interest than either the sur-
⑦ rounding pedestrian streets or the **Musée du Vieux Nîmes** (Museum of Old Nîmes), housed opposite the cathedral in the 17th-century Bishop's Palace. Embroidered garments and woolen shawls fill the rooms in an exotic and vibrant display. Nîmes used to be a cloth-manufacturing center and lent its name to what has become one of the world's most popular fabrics—denim (*de Nîmes*—from Nîmes). *Pl. aux Herbes, tel. 66–36–00–64. Admission free. Open daily 10–6.*

Head right from the cathedral along rue des Halles, then left
⑧ down rue du Général-Perrier, to reach the **Maison Carrée.** Despite its name (the "square house"), this is an oblong Roman temple, dating from the 1st century AD. Transformed down the ages into a stable, a private dwelling, a town hall, and a church, today the building is a museum that contains an imposing statue of Apollo and other antiquities. The exquisite carvings along the cornice and on the Corinthian capitals rank as some of the finest in Roman architecture. Thomas Jefferson admired the Maison Carrée's chaste lines of columns so much that he had them copied for the Virginia state capitol at Richmond. *Blvd. Victor-Hugo. Admission free. Open mid-June–mid-Sept., daily 9–7; mid-Sept.–Oct. and Apr.–mid-June, daily 9–noon and 2–6; Nov.–Mar., daily 9–noon and 2–5.*

Rue Molière and rue Boissier lead from the Maison Carrée to
⑨ the **Jardin de la Fontaine.** This elaborate, formal garden was landscaped on the site of the Roman baths in the 18th century, when the Source de Nemausus, a once-sacred spring, was channeled into pools and a canal. Close by, you'll see the shattered
⑩ remnant of a Roman ruin, known as the **Temple of Diana.** At the
⑪ far end of the jardin is the **Tour Magne**—a stumpy tower that was probably used as a lookout post, which, despite having lost 30 feet during the course of time, still provides fine views of Nîmes for anyone who is energetic enough to climb the 140 steps to the top. *Quai de la Fontaine, tel. 66–67–65–56. Admission to Tour Magne: 10 frs.; joint ticket as above. Open mid-June–mid-Sept., daily 9–7; mid-Sept.–Oct. and Apr.–mid-June, daily 9–noon and 2–6; Nov.–Mar., daily 9–noon and 2–5.*

⑫ Both N113 and the A9 expressway link Nîmes to **Montpellier,** 50 kilometers (30 miles) southwest. Montpellier is a comparatively young town, a mere 1,000 years old; no Romans settled here. Ever since medieval times, Montpellier's reputation has been linked to its university, which was founded in the 14th century. Its medical school, in particular, was so highly esteemed that François Rabelais, one of France's top 16th-century writers, left his native Loire Valley to take his doctorate here. Montpellier remains one of France's premier universities, and a student population of 20,000 peps things up during the school year.

The 17th-century town center has been improved by an imaginative urban planning program, and several streets and squares are now banned to cars. The heart of Montpellier is place de la Comédie, a wide square now free of traffic jams, much to the benefit of the cafés and terraces laid out before the handsome 19th-century facade of the civic theater.

Boulevard Sarrail leads from the far end of the square, past the leafy Esplanade with its rows of plane trees, to the **Musée Fabre.** The museum's collection of art highlights important works by Gustave Courbet (notably *Bonjour Monsieur Courbet*) and Eugène Delacroix *(Femmes d'Alger)*, as well as paintings by Frédéric Bazille (1841–70)—whose death during the Franco-Prussian War deprived Impressionism of one of its earliest exponents. Older standouts of the museum's varied collection include pictures from the English (Joshua Reynolds), Italian (Raphael), Flemish (David Teniers), and Spanish (Jusepe de Ribera) schools. *37 blvd. Sarrail, tel. 67–66–06–34. Admission: 16 frs. (free Wed.). Open Tues.–Sat. 9–5:30.*

Follow rue Montpelliéret, alongside the museum, into the heart of old Montpellier—a maze of crooked, bustling streets ideal for shopping and strolling. Rue Foch strikes a more disciplined note, slicing straight through to the pride of Montpellier, the **Promenade du Peyrou.** With its wrought-iron railings and majestic flights of steps, this long, broad, tree-shaded terrace has great style. An equestrian statue of Louis XIV rides triumphant, and at the far end carved friezes and columns mask a water tower. Water used to arrive along the **St-Clément aqueduct,** an imposing two-tiered structure 70 feet high and nearly 1,000 yards long. Locals still cluster beneath the aqueduct's arches to drink pastis and play boules.

Just down boulevard Henri IV from the Promenade du Peyrou is France's oldest **botanical garden,** planted by order of Henri IV in 1593. Horticulture buffs will admire the exceptional range of plants, flowers, and trees that grow here, and even nongardeners will appreciate this oasis of peace, where water lilies float among the lotus flowers. *Admission free. Gardens open daily 9–noon and 2–5. Greenhouses open weekdays 9–noon and 2–5, Sat. 9–noon.*

The arid, rocky Midi landscape begins to change as you head southeast from Montpellier along D21, past pools and lagoons, ❸ to **La Grande Motte,** the most lavish—and, some would say, ugliest—of a string of new resorts built along the Languedoc coast. The mosquitoes that once infested this watery area have finally been vanquished, and tourists have taken their place. La Grande Motte was only a glint in an architect's eye back in the late '60s; since then, its arresting pyramid-shape apartment blocks have influenced several French resorts. They host thousands of vacationers each year.

Time Out   Thousands of tons of oysters are cultivated in the nearby Etang (lagoon) de Thau; many end up featured on the menu of the elegant **Alexandre-Amirauté.** You can eat your oysters amid impressive Louis XV surroundings while gazing out over the clear blue waters of the Mediterranean. *345 esplanade Maurice-Justin.*

⓮ Thirteen kilometers (8 miles) farther east is **Aigues-Mortes,** an astonishing relic of medieval town planning, created at the behest of Louis IX (St-Louis) in the 13th century. Medieval streets are usually crooked and higgledy-piggledy; at Aigues-Mortes, however, a grid plan was adopted, hemmed in by sturdy walls sprouting towers at regular intervals. Aigues-Mortes was originally a port, and Louis used it as a base for his crusades to the Holy Land. The sea has long since receded, though, and Aigues-Mortes's size and importance have decreased with it.

Unlike most of the medieval buildings, the **fortifications** remain intact. Walk along the top of the city walls and admire some remarkable views across the town and salt marshes. You can also explore the powerful **Tour de Constance,** originally designed as a fortress-keep and used in the 18th century as a prison for Protestants who refused to convert to official state Catholicism. One such unfortunate, Marie Durand, languished here for 38 years. Abraham Mazel was luckier. He spent 10 months chiseling a hole in the wall, while his companions sang psalms to distract the jailers. The ruse worked: Mazel and 16 others escaped. *Admission: 24 frs. adults, 13 frs. students and senior citizens, 5 frs. children. Tower and ramparts open Apr.–Oct., daily 9–7; Nov.–Mar. 9:30–noon and 2–5:30.*

Head east on D58 across the haunting, desolate **Camargue:** a marshy wilderness of endless horizons, vast pools, low flat plains, and, overhead, innumerable species of migrating birds. The Camargue is formed by the sprawling Rhône delta and extends over 300 square miles. Much of it is untouched by man; this is a land of black bulls and sturdy, free-roaming gray horses. There are just two towns worthy of the name: Aigues-Mortes and, 32 kilometers (20 miles) southeast via D58/D570, Saintes-Maries-de-la-Mer.

⓯ **Stes-Maries-de-la-Mer** is a commercialized resort, mainly frequented by British tourists in search of the Camargue's principal sandy beach. Its tiny, dark fortress-church houses caskets containing relics of the "Holy Maries" after whom the town is named. Legend has it that Mary Jacobi (the sister of the Virgin), Mary Magdalene, Mary Salome (mother of the apostles James and John), and their black servant Sarah were washed up here around AD 40 after being abandoned at sea—why, no one knows. Their adopted town rapidly became a site of pilgrimage, the most important site for Gypsies. Sarah was adopted as their patron saint, and to this day, Gypsies from all over Europe and the rest of the world stage colorful pilgrimages to Stes-Maries in late May and late October, while guitar-strumming pseudogypsies serenade rich-looking tourists throughout the summer.

Take D85-A north from Stes-Maries through the 30-acre **Parc Ornithologique,** itself part of the vast Réserve Nationale centered on the Etang (lagoon) de Vaccarès. The Parc Ornithologique offers a protected environment to vegetation and wildlife: Birds from northern Europe and Siberia spend the winter here, while pink flamingoes flock in during the summer months. *Admission: 23 frs. Open Mar.–Oct., daily 8–dusk.*

⓰ Continue along D85-A until it rejoins D570, then keep north on this road for 25 kilometers (16 miles) until you reach **Arles.** The first inhabitants of Arles were probably the Greeks, who arrived from Marseille in the 6th century BC. The Romans, however, left a stronger mark, constructing the theater and amphitheater (Arènes) that remain Arles's biggest tourist attractions. Arles used to be a thriving port before the Mediterranean receded over what is now the marshy Camargue. It was also the site of the southernmost bridge over the Rhône, and became a commercial crossroads; merchants from as far afield as Arabia, Assyria, and Africa would linger here to do business on their way from Rome to Spain or northern Europe.

Firebrand Dutchman Vincent Van Gogh produced much of his best work—and chopped off his ear—in Arles during a frenzied 15-month spell (1888–90) just before his suicide at 37. Unfortunately, the houses he lived in are no longer standing—they were destroyed during World War II—but one of his most famous subjects remains: the **Pont de Trinquetaille** across the Rhône. Van Gogh's rendering of the bridge, painted in 1888, was auctioned a century later for $20 million.

Local art museums, such as the **Musée Réattu**, 300 yards from the bridge along quai Marx-Dormoy, can't compete with that type of bidding—which is one reason none of Van Gogh's works are displayed there. Another is that Arles failed to appreciate Van Gogh; he was jeered at and eventually packed off to the nearest lunatic asylum. To add insult to injury, Jacques Réattu, after whom the museum is named, was a local painter of dazzling mediocrity. His works fill three rooms, but of much greater interest is the collection of modern drawings and paintings by Pablo Picasso, Fernand Léger, and Maurice de Vlaminck, as well as the photography section containing images by some of the field's leading names. *Rue du Grand-Prieuré, tel. 90–96–37–68. Admission: 15 frs.; joint ticket to all monuments and museums: 44 frs. adults, 31 frs. students and senior citizens, children free. Open June–Sept., daily 9:30–7; Nov.–Mar., daily 10–12:30 and 2–5; Apr.–May and Oct., daily 9:30–12:30 and 2–6.*

The museum facade, facing the Rhône, dates from the Middle Ages and formed part of a 15th-century priory. Beside it are the ruins of the **Palais Constantin** (same opening times as above), site of Provence's largest Roman baths, the **Thèrmes de la Trouille** (entrance on rue Dominique-Maisto; admission: 12 francs; joint ticket as above).

Most of the significant sights and museums in Arles are set well away from the Rhône. The most notable is the 26,000-capacity **Arènes,** built in the 1st century AD to showcase circuses and fight-to-the-death gladiator combats. The amphitheater is 150 yards long and as wide as a football field, with each of its two stories composed of 60 arches; the original top tier has long since crumbled, and the three square towers were added in the Middle Ages. Climb to the upper story for some satisfying views across the town and countryside. Despite its venerable age, the amphitheater still sees a lot of action, mainly Sunday afternoon bullfights. *Rond-Point des Arènes, tel. 90–96–03–70. Admission: 17 frs.; joint ticket as above. Open June–Sept., daily 8:30–7; Nov.–Mar., daily 9–noon and 2–4:30; Apr.–May and Oct., daily 9–12:30 and 2–6:30.*

Just 100 yards from the Arènes are the scanty remains of Arles's **Théâtre Antique** (Roman theater); the bits of marble column scattered around the grassy enclosure hint poignantly at the theater's onetime grandeur. The capacity may have shrunk from 7,000 to a few hundred, but the orchestra pit and a few tiers of seats are still used for the city's Music and Drama festival each July. *Rue du Cloître, tel. 90–96–93–30 for ticket information. Admission: 12 frs.; joint ticket as above. Open June–Sept., daily 8:30–7; Nov.–Mar., daily 9–noon and 2–4:30; Apr.–May and Oct., daily 9–12:30 and 2–6:30.*

Follow rue de la Calade to place de la République. To the left is the church of **St-Trophime,** dating mainly from the 11th and 12th centuries; subsequent additions have not spoiled its architectural harmony. Take time to admire the accomplished 12th-century sculptures flanking the main portal, featuring the Last Judgment, the apostles, the Nativity, and various saints. There are other well-crafted sculptures in the cloisters. *Rue de l'Hôtel-de-Ville. Admission to cloisters: 21 frs.; joint ticket as above. Open June–Sept., daily 8:30–7; Nov.–Mar., daily 9–noon and 2–4:30; Apr.–May and Oct., daily 9–12:30 and 2–6:30.*

Opposite St-Trophime is the **Musée d'Art Païen** (Museum of Pagan Art), housed in a former church next to the 17th-century Hôtel de Ville (Town Hall). The "pagan art" displays encompass Roman statues, busts, mosaics, and a white marble sarcophagus. You'll also see a copy of the famous statue the *Venus of Arles;* Sun King Louis XIV waltzed off to the Louvre with the original. *Pl. de la République, tel. 90–49–36–97. Admission: 12 frs.; joint ticket as above. Open June–Sept., daily 8:30–7; Nov.–Mar., daily 9–noon and 2–4:30; Apr.–May and Oct., 9–12:30 and 2–6:30.*

Turn left alongside the Hôtel de Ville into plan de la Cour. A hundred yards down, in a former 17th-century Jesuit chapel, is the **Musée d'Art Chrétien** (Museum of Christian Art). One of the highlights is a magnificent collection of sculpted marble sarcophagi, second only to the Vatican's, that date from the 4th century on. Downstairs, you can explore a vast double gallery built in the 1st century BC as a grain store and see part of the great Roman sewer built two centuries later. *Rue Balze. Admission: 12 frs.; joint ticket as above. Open June–Sept., daily 8:30–7; Nov.–Mar., daily 9–noon and 2–4:30; Apr.–May and Oct., daily 9–12:30 and 2–6:30.*

The **Museon Arlaten,** an old-fashioned folklore museum, is housed next door in a 16th-century mansion. The charming displays include costumes and headdresses, puppets, and waxworks, lovingly assembled by that great 19th-century Provençal poet Frédéric Mistral. *29 rue de la République, tel. 90–96–08–23. Admission: 12 frs.; joint ticket as above. Open June–Sept., daily 8:30–7; Nov.–Mar., Tues.–Sun. 9–noon and 2–4:30; Apr.–May and Oct., Tues.–Sun. 9–12:30 and 2–6:30.*

Head down rue du Président-Wilson opposite the museum to the **boulevard des Luces,** a broad, leafy avenue flanked by trendy shops and sidewalk cafés. Locals favor it for leisurely strolls and aperitifs.

At the east end of the boulevard is the **Jardin d'Hiver,** a public garden whose fountains figure in several of Van Gogh's paintings. Cross the gardens to rue Fassin and head left to place de la Croisière and the start of the allée des Sarcophages, which leads to the **Alyscamps,** a Provençal term meaning "mythical burial ground." This was a prestigious burial site from Roman times through the Middle Ages. A host of important finds have been excavated here, many of which are exhibited in the town's museums. Empty tombs and sarcophagi line the allée des Sarcophages, creating a powerfully gloomy atmosphere in dull weather.

⑰ Leave Arles on Avignon-bound N570, and almost immediately turn right along D17 to the striking village of **Fontvieille,** 10 kilometers (6 miles) away and home of the **Moulin de Daudet.** Nineteenth-century author Alphonse Daudet dreamed up his short stories, *Lettres de Mon Moulin,* in this well-preserved, charmingly situated windmill just up D33 on the outskirts of the village. Inside there's a small museum devoted to Daudet, and you can walk upstairs to see the original grain-grinding system. *Tel. 90–54–60–78. Admission: 8 frs. adults, 4 frs. children. Open Apr.–Oct., daily 9–noon and 2–7; Nov.–Dec. and Feb.–Mar., daily 10–noon and 2–5; Jan., Sun. only, 10–noon and 2–5.*

⑱ From Fontvieille, take D17 and then D78-A to **Les Baux-de-Provence,** 8 kilometers (5 miles) farther. Les Baux-de-Provence is an amazing place, perched on a mighty spur of rock high above the surrounding countryside of vines, olive trees, and quarries. The mineral bauxite was discovered here in 1821. Half of Les Baux is composed of tiny climbing streets and ancient stone houses inhabited, for the most part, by local craftsmen selling pottery, carvings, and assorted knickknacks. The other half, the Ville Morte (Dead Town), is a mass of medieval ruins, vestiges of Les Baux's glorious past, when the town boasted 6,000 inhabitants and the defensive impregnability of its rocky site far outweighed its isolation and poor access.

Cars must be left in the parking lot at the entrance to the village. Close to the 12th-century church of St-Vincent (where local shepherds continue an age-old tradition by herding their lambs to midnight mass at Christmas) is the 16th-century **Hôtel des Porcelets,** featuring some 18th-century frescoes and a small but choice collection of contemporary art. *Pl. St-Vincent. Admission: 20 frs. (joint ticket with Musée Lapidaire and Ville Morte). Open Easter–Oct., daily 9–noon and 2–6.*

Rue Neuve leads around to the **Ville Morte.** Enter through the 14th-century Tour-de-Brau, which houses the Musée Lapidaire, displaying locally excavated sculptures and ceramics. You can wander at will amid the rocks and ruins of the Dead Town. A 13th-century castle stands at one end of the clifftop and, at the other, the Tour Paravelle and the Monument Charloun Rieu. From here, you can enjoy a magnificent view of Arles and the Camargue as far as Stes-Maries-de-la-Mer. *Ville Morte. Admission: 20 frs. (joint ticket with museums). Open daily 9–noon and 2–6.*

Half a mile north of Les Baux, off D27, is the **Cathédrale d'Images,** where the majestic setting of the old Baux quarries, with their towering rock faces and stone pillars, is used as a colossal screen for nature-based film shows (Jacques Cousteau gets frequent billing). *Rte. de Maillane, tel. 90–54–38–65. Admission: 35 frs. adults, 20 frs. children. Open mid-Feb.–mid-Nov., daily 10–7.*

Hilly D5 heads 8 kilometers (5 miles) north from Les Baux to
the small town of **St-Rémy de Provence,** founded in the 6th century BC and known as Glanum to the Romans. St-Rémy is renowned for its outstanding Roman remains: Temples, baths,
forum, and houses have been excavated, while the Mausoleum
and Arc Municipal (Triumphal Arch) welcome visitors as they
enter the town.

The **Roman Mausoleum** was erected around AD 100 to the mem-
ory of Caius and Lucius Caesar, grandsons of the emperor Augustus; the four bas-reliefs around its base, depicting ancient
battle scenes, are stunningly preserved. The Mausoleum is
composed of four archways topped by a circular colonnade. The
nearby **Arc Municipal** is a few decades older and has suffered
heavily; the upper half has crumbled away, although you can
still make out some of the stone carvings.

Excavations since 1921 have uncovered about a tenth of the site
of the adjacent Roman town. Many of the finds—statues, pottery, and jewelry—can be examined at the town museum, **Le
Musée Archéologique,** in the center of St-Rémy. *Hôtel de Sade,
rue Parage, tel. 90–92–13–07. Admission: 12 frs. adults, 6 frs.
children. Open June–Oct., daily 9–noon and 2–6; Apr.–May
and Oct., weekends 10–noon, weekdays 3–6; closed Nov.–Mar.*

Opposite the Hôtel de Sade, in a grand 16th-century mansion,
is the **Musée des Alpilles.** It boasts a fine collection of minerals
found in the nearby hills (the Alpilles), plus items of regional
folklore: costumes, furniture, and figurines. Exhibits also
touch on the 16th-century astrologer Nostradamus, who was
born in St-Rémy (his house can be seen on the other side of the
church, on rue Hoche, but it's not open to the public). *Pl.
Favier. Admission: 12 frs. Open Apr.–Oct., Wed.–Mon. 10–
noon and 2–6; Mar. and Nov., weekends 10–noon and 2–4;
closed Dec.–Feb.*

Take D99 16 kilometers (10 miles) west from St-Rémy to
Tarascon, home of the mythical Tarasque, a monster that would
emerge from the Rhône to gobble children and cattle. Luckily
Ste-Martha, washed up with the three Maries at Stes-Maries-
de-la-Mer, allegedly tamed the beast with a sprinkle of holy
water, after which the inhabitants clobbered it senseless and
slashed it to pieces. This dramatic event is celebrated on the
last Sunday in June with a colorful parade.

Ever since the 12th century, Tarascon has possessed a formida-
ble **castle** to protect it from any beast or man that might be
tempted to emulate the Tarasque's fiendish deeds. The castle's
massive stone walls, towering 150 feet above the rocky banks
of the Rhône, are among the most daunting in France, so it's
not surprising that the castle was used as a prison for centuries. Since 1926, however, the chapels, vaulted royal apartments, and stone carvings of the interior have been restored
to less-intimidating glory. *Tel. 90–91–01–93. Admission: 24
frs. adults, 13 frs. senior citizens, 5 frs. children. Open July
and Aug., daily 9–7; Sept.–June, guided tours only 9–11 and
2–6 (last tour at 5 in Apr. and May; at 4, Oct.–Mar.).*

It's just 24 kilometers (15 miles) from Tarascon to Avignon and
the start of our second tour.

Tour 2: The Vaucluse

㉑ A warren of medieval alleys nestling behind a protective ring of stocky towers, **Avignon** is possibly best known for its Pont St-Bénezet, the Avignon bridge that many will remember singing about during their nursery-rhyme days. No one dances across the bridge these days, however; it's amputated in midstream, and has been ever since the 17th century, when a cataclysmic storm washed half of it away. Still, Avignon has lots to offer, starting with the Palais des Papes (Papal Palace), where seven exiled popes camped between 1309 and 1377 after fleeing from the corruption of Rome. Avignon remained papal property until 1791, and elegant mansions and a then-population of 80,000 bear witness to the town's 18th-century prosperity.

Numbers in the margin correspond to points of interest on the Avignon map.

㉒ Avignon's main street, rue de la République, leads from the tourist office (41 cours Jean-Jaurès) past shops and cafés to place de l'Horloge and place du Palais, site of the colossal **Palais des Papes.**This "palace" creates a disconcertingly fortresslike impression, underlined by the austerity of its interior decor; most of the furnishings were dispersed during the French Revolution. Some imagination is required to picture it in medieval splendor, awash with color and worldly clerics enjoying what the 14th-century Italian poet Petrarch called "licentious banquets."

On close inspection, two different styles of building emerge: the severe **Palais Vieux** (Old Palace), built between 1334 and 1342 by Pope Benedict XII, a member of the Cistercian order, which frowned on frivolity, and the more decorative **Palais Nouveau** (New Palace), built in the following decade by the arty, lavish-living Pope Clement VI. The Great Court, where visitors arrive, forms a link between the two.

The main rooms of the Palais Vieux are the consistory (council hall), decorated with some excellent 14th-century frescoes by Simone Martini; the Chapelle St-Jean (original frescoes by Matteo Giovanetti); the Grand Tinel, or Salle des Festins, with a majestic vaulted roof and a series of 18th-century Gobelin tapestries; the Chapelle St-Martial (more Matteo frescoes); the Chambre du Cerf, with a richly decorated ceiling, murals featuring a stag hunt, and a delightful view of Avignon; the Chambre de Parement (papal antechamber); and the Chambre à Coucher (papal bedchamber).

The principal attractions of the Palais Nouveau are the Grande Audience, a magnificent two-nave hall on the ground floor, and, upstairs, the Chapelle Clémentine, where the college of cardinals gathered to elect the new pope. *Pl. du Palais des Papes, tel. 90–86–03–32. Admission: 32 frs. adults, 16 frs. students, children free. Guided tours only Mar.–Oct. Open Easter–June, daily 9–12:15 and 2–5:15; July–Sept., daily 9–6; Oct.–Easter, daily 9–11:30 and 2–5.*

㉓ The 12th-century **cathedral** nearby contains the Gothic tomb of
㉔ Pope John XII. Beyond is the **Rocher des Doms,** a large, attractive garden offering fine views of Avignon, the Rhône, and the
㉕ celebrated **Pont St-Bénezet**—built, according to legend, by a local shepherd named Bénezet in the 12th century. It was the first bridge to span the Rhône at Avignon and was originally

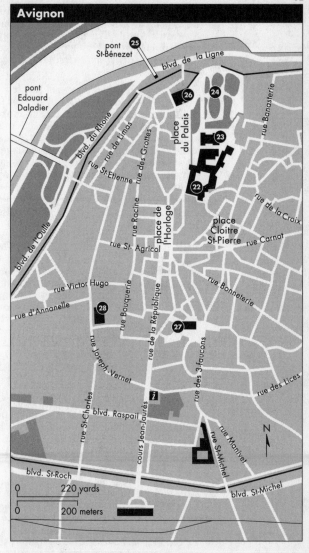

Avignon

900 yards long. Though only half the bridge remains, it's worth strolling along for the views and a visit to the tiny Chapelle St-Nicolas that juts out over the river.

26 The medieval **Petit Palais,** situated between the bridge and the Rocher des Doms garden, was once home to cardinals and archbishops. Nowadays it contains an outstanding collection of Old Masters, led by the Italian schools of Venice, Siena, and Florence (note Sandro Botticelli's *Virgin and Child*). *21 pl. du Paais, tel. 90–86–44–58. Admission: 18 frs. adults, 9 frs. children; free Sun. Open Wed.–Mon. 9:30–noon and 2–6.*

Double back past the Papal Palace and venture into the narrow, winding, shop-lined streets of old Avignon. Halfway down

㉗ rue de la République is the **Musée Lapidaire,** which displays a variety of archaeological finds—including the remains of Avignon's Arc de Triomphe—in a sturdy 17th-century Baroque chapel fronted by an imposing facade. *27 rue de la République. Admission: 10 frs. adults, children free. Open daily noon–7.*

㉘ Cross rue de la République and turn right into rue Joseph-Vernet. A few minutes' walk will lead you to the **Musée Calvet,** an 18th-century town house featuring an extensive collection of mainly French paintings from the 16th century on; highlights include works by Théodore Géricault, Camille Corot, Édouard Manet, Raoul Dufy, Maurice de Vlaminck, and the Italian artist Amedeo Modigliani. Greek, Roman, and Etruscan statuettes are also displayed. *65 rue Joseph-Vernet, tel. 90–86–33–84. At press time the museum was closed for renovation, and its reopening was still unscheduled.*

Numbers in the margin correspond to points of interest on the Provence map.

㉙ From Avignon, head north to Orange. The most picturesque route, via N7/D17, goes by the hillside village of **Château-neuf-du-Pape,** founded by the popes in the 14th century. The popes knew their wine: The vineyard here is still regarded as the best of the southern Rhône, even though the vines are embedded less in soil than in stones and pebbles. Several producers stage tastings in the village and sell distinctive wine bottles emblazoned with the crossed-key papal crest.

Time Out Inexpensive local wines, filling fare, and a cheerful welcome make **La Mule du Pape** a good choice for lunch. *23 pl. Change. Closed Tues.*

㉚ **Orange,** 10 kilometers (6 miles) north of Châteauneuf via D68, is a small, pleasant town that sinks into total siesta somnolence during hot afternoons but, at other times, buzzes with visitors who are keen on admiring its Roman remains.

The magnificent, semicircular **Théâtre Antique,** in the center of town, is the best-preserved remains of a theater from the ancient world. It was built just before the birth of Christ, to the same dimensions as that of Arles. Orange's theater, however, has a mighty screen-wall, over 100 yards long and 120 feet high, and steeply climbing terraces carved into the hillside. Seven thousand spectators can crowd in, and regularly do, for open-air concerts and operatic performances; the acoustics are superb. This is the only Roman theater that still possesses its original Imperial statue, of Caesar Augustus, which stands in the middle of the screen. At nearly 12 feet, it's one of the tallest Roman statues in existence. *Pl. des Frères-Mounet, tel. 90–51–17–60. Admission: 22 frs.; joint ticket with Musée Municipal. Open Apr.–Oct., daily 9–6:30; Nov.–Mar., daily 10–noon and 1:30–5.*

The **Parc de la Colline St-Eutrope,** the banked garden behind the theater, yields a fine view of the theater and of the 6,000-foot Mont Ventoux to the east. Walk up cours Aristide-Briand, turn right at the top, then left immediately after to the venerable **Arc de Triomphe**—composed of a large central arch flanked by two smaller ones, the whole topped by a massive entablature. The 70-foot arch, the third-highest Roman arch still standing, towered over the old Via Agrippa between Arles and Lyon and was probably built around AD 25 in honor of the Gallic Wars. The carvings on the north side depict the legionaries' battles with the Gauls and Caesar's naval showdown with the ships of Marseille. Today the arch presides over a busy traffic circle.

The D975 heads 27 kilometers (17 miles) northeast from Orange to **Vaison-la-Romaine.** As its name suggests, Vaison was also a Roman town. The remains here are more extensive, though less spectacular than those at Orange; they can be explored on either side of the avenue du Général-de-Gaulle. The floors and walls of houses, villas, a basilica, and a theater have been unearthed, and the Roman street plan is partly discernible. Statues and objects are housed in a small museum near the theater. With its lush lawns and colorful flower beds, the entire site suggests a well-tended historical garden. *Admission to remains and museum: 26 frs. adults, 15 frs. students and senior citizens. Open Apr.–Oct., daily 9–7; Nov.–Mar., daily 9–5.*

Before leaving Vaison, pause to admire the 2,000-year-old Roman bridge over the River Ouvèze and venture briefly into the medieval town across the river. Then head 10 kilometers (6 miles) south along D938 to **Malaucène,** at the foot of **Mont Ventoux**—a huge mountain that looms incongruously above the surrounding plains. Weather conditions on this sprawling, whalelike bulk—known reverentially as "Le" Ventoux—can vary dramatically. In summer, few places in France experience such scorching heat; in winter, the Ventoux's snow-topped peak recalls the Alps. Its arid heights sometimes provide a grueling setting for the Tour de France cycling race; British bicyclist Tommy Simpson collapsed and died under the Ventoux's pitiless sun in 1967.

D974 winds its way from Malaucène up to the summit, 6,250 feet above sea level. Stay on D974 as it doubles back around the southern slopes of the Ventoux, then follow it southwest from Bédoin toward Carpentras. From here, take D938 south to **L'Isle-sur-la-Sorgue,** 18 kilometers (11 miles) away, where the River Sorgue splits into a number of channels and once turned the waterwheels of the town's silk factories. Silk worms were cultivated locally, one reason for the profusion of mulberry trees in Provence (mulberry leaves being a silkworm's favorite food). Some of the waterwheels are still in place, and you can admire them as you stroll along the banks of the river that encircles the town. The richly decorated 17th-century church is also of interest.

Time Out   A good place for lunch is **Le Pescador,** an inexpensive restaurant whose shaded terrace overlooks the arms of the Sorgue. There is a wide choice and an excellent-value menu during the week. *Le Partage des Eaux. Closed Mon.*

Tiny D25 leads east from L'Isle-sur-la-Sorgue to **Fontaine-de-Vaucluse,** 8 kilometers (5 miles) away. The "fountain" in question is the site of the River Sorgue's emergence from underground imprisonment: Water shoots up from a cavern as the emerald-green river sprays and cascades at the foot of steep cliffs. This is the picture in springtime or after heavy rains; in the drought of summer, the scene may be less spectacular and infested with tourists.

It's just 6 kilometers (4 miles) from Fontaine-de-Vaucluse to
③⑤ **Gordes** as the crow flies, but drivers have to wind their way
south, east, and then north for 16 kilometers (10 miles) on
D100-A, D100, D2, and D15 to skirt the impassable hillside.
The golden-stone village of Gordes is perched dramatically on
its own hill. At the summit sits a Renaissance **château** with a
collection of mind-stretching, geometric-patterned paintings
by 20th-century Hungarian-French artist Victor Vasarely. *Tel.
90–72–02–89. Admission: 20 frs. adults, 12 frs. students and
senior citizens, children free. Open Wed.–Mon. 10–noon and
2–6; closed Tues.*

In a wild valley some 4 kilometers (2 miles) north of Gordes (via
D177) stands the beautiful 12th-century **Abbey of Sénanque.** In
1969, its Cistercian monks moved to the island of St-Honorat
(*see* Chapter 4), off the shore of Cannes, and the admirably
preserved buildings here are now a cultural center that presents concerts and exhibitions. The dormitory, refectory,
church, and chapter house can be visited, along with an odd
museum devoted to the Sahara's Tuareg nomads. *Tel. 90–72–
05–72. Admission: 15 frs. Open July and Aug., Mon.–Sat.
10–7, Sun. 2–7; Sept.–June, Mon.–Sat. 10–noon and 2–6,
Sun. 2–6.*

Return to Gordes and strike 10 kilometers (6 miles) east along
③⑥ D2/D102 to another hilltop village, **Roussillon,** whose houses
are built with a distinctive orange-and pink-colored stone. This
is ocher country, and local quarrying has slashed cliffs into
③⑦ bizarre shapes. **Bonnieux,** 11 kilometers (7 miles) south of
Roussillon (D149), is equally picturesque. Climb to the terrace
of the old church (not to be confused with the big 19th-century
one lower down) for a sweeping view north that takes in
Gordes, Roussillon, and the nearby château of Lacoste, now in
ruins but once home to that notorious aristocrat the marquis de
Sade.

Time Out   The setting of the **Prieuré**—a charming old priory in the pretty
hilltop village of Bonnieux—is its main appeal. The simple Provençal dishes are made memorable by the accompanying panoramic views. *Rue Aurard. Closed Tues. and Thurs. lunch.*

Aix-en-Provence, starting point for our third tour, lies 48 kilometers (29 miles) southeast.

Tour 3: The Marseille Area

Many villages, but few towns, are as well preserved as the tra-
③⑧ ditional capital of Provence: elegant **Aix-en-Provence**. The Romans were drawn here by the presence of thermal springs; the
name Aix originates from *Aquae Sextiae* (the waters of
Sextius) in honor of the consul who reputedly founded the town
in 122 BC. Twenty years later, a vast army of Germanic barbari-
ans invaded the region but were defeated by General Marius at
a neighboring mountain, known ever since as the Montagne
Sainte-Victoire. Marius remains a popular local first name to
this day.

Aix-en-Provence numbers two of France's most creative ge-
niuses among its sons: the Impressionist Paul Cézanne (1839–
1906), many of whose paintings feature the nearby countryside, especially Montagne Sainte-Victoire (though Cézanne

would not recognize it now, after the forest fire that ravaged its slopes in 1990), and the novelist Émile Zola (1840–1902), who, in several of his works, described Aix (as "Plassans") and his boyhood friendship with Cézanne.

The celebrated **cours Mirabeau,** flanked with intertwining plane trees, is the town's nerve center, a gracious, lively avenue with the feel of a toned-down, intimate Champs-Elysées. It divides old Aix into two, with narrow medieval streets to the north and sophisticated, haughty 18th-century mansions to the south. Begin your visit at the west end of cours Mirabeau (the tourist office is close by at 2 place de la Libération). Halfway down is the **Fontaine des Neuf Canons** (Fountain of the Nine Cannons), dating from 1691, and farther along is the **Fontaine d'Eau Thermale** (Thermal Water), built in 1734.

Any route through the quaint pedestrian streets of the old town, north of cours Mirabeau, is rewarding. Wend your way up to the **Cathédrale St-Sauveur.** Its mishmash of styles lacks harmony, and the interior feels gloomy and dilapidated, but you may want to inspect the remarkable 15th-century triptych by Nicolas Froment, entitled *Tryptique du Buisson Ardent (Burning Bush),* depicting King René (duke of Anjou, count of Provence, and titular king of Sicily) and Queen Joan kneeling beside the Virgin. Ask the sacristan to spotlight it for you (he'll expect a tip) and to remove the protective shutters from the ornate 16th-century carvings on the cathedral portals. Afterward, wander into the tranquil Romanesque cloisters next door to admire the carved pillars and slender colonnades.

The adjacent Archbishop's Palace is home to the **Musée des Tapisseries** (Tapestry Museum). Its highlight is a magnificent suite of 17 tapestries made in Beauvais that date, like the palace itself, from the 17th and 18th centuries. Nine woven panels illustrate the adventures of the bumbling Don Quixote. *28 pl. des Martyrs de la Résistance, tel. 42–23–09–91. Admission: 12 frs. Open Wed.–Mon. 10–noon and 2–6.*

Return past the cathedral and take rue de la Roque up to the broad, leafy boulevard that encircles Old Aix. Head up avenue Pasteur, opposite, then turn right into avenue Paul-Cézanne, which leads to the **Musée-Atelier de Paul Cézanne** (Cézanne's studio). Cézanne's pioneering work, with its interest in angular forms, paved the way for the Cubist style of the early 20th century. No major pictures are on display here, but his studio remains as he left it at the time of his death in 1906, scattered with the great man's pipe, clothing, and other personal possessions, many of which he painted in his still lifes. *9 av. Paul-Cézanne, tel. 42–21–06–53. Admission: 12.50 frs. adults, 6 frs. senior citizens and children. Open Wed.–Mon. 10–noon and 2:30–6; closed Tues.*

Time Out Good addresses for picnic provisions are the **Olivier** *charcuterie* (rue Jacques-de-la-Roque near the cathedral) and the **Brémond** *patisserie* (36 cours Mirabeau, on the corner of rue du Quatre-Septembre).

Make your way back to cours Mirabeau and cross into the southern half of Aix. The streets here are straight and rationally planned, flanked with symmetrical mansions imbued with classical elegance. Rue du Quatre-Septembre, three-quarters of the way down cours Mirabeau, leads to the splendid **Fontaine**

des Quatre Dauphins, where sculpted dolphins play in a fountain erected in 1667. Turn left along rue Cardinale to the **Musée Granet,** named after another of Aix's artistic sons: François Granet (1775–1849), whose works are good examples of the formal, at times sentimental, style of art popular during the first half of the 19th century. Granet's paintings show none of the fervor of Cézanne, who is represented here with several oils and watercolors. An impressive collection of European paintings from the 16th to the 19th century, plus archaeological finds from Egypt, Greece, and the Roman Empire, complete the museum's collections. *13 rue Cardinale, tel. 42–38–14–70. Admission: 14 frs. Open Wed.–Mon. 10–noon and 2–6; closed Tues.*

The quickest, most effective route by car between Aix and Marseille is the toll-free A51 expressway, provided you avoid the heavy morning and evening rush-hour traffic.

㊵ Marseille is not crowded with tourist goodies, nor is its reputation as a big dirty city entirely unjustified, but it still has more going for it than many realize: a craggy mountain hinterland that provides a spectacular backdrop, superb coastal views of nearby islands, and the sights and smells of a Mediterranean melting pot where different peoples have mingled for centuries—ever since the Phocaean Greeks invaded in around 600 BC. The most recent immigrants come from North Africa.

Numbers in the margin correspond to points of interest on the Marseille map.

Marseille is the Mediterranean's largest port. The sizable, ugly industrial docks virtually rub shoulders with the intimate, pic
㊵ turesque old harbor, the **Vieux Port,** packed with fishing boats and pleasure craft: This is the heart of Marseille, with the Canebière avenue leading down to the water's edge.

Pick up your leaflets and town plan at the tourist office (4 La Canebière) and peruse them on a café terrace overlooking the Vieux Port. Until the mid-19th century, this was the center of maritime activity in Marseille. These days, a forest of yacht and fishing-boat masts creates an impression of colorful bustle. Restaurants line the quays, and fishwives spout incomprehensible Provençal insults as they serve gleaming fresh sardines each morning. The Marseillais can be an irascible lot: Louis XIV built the Fort St-Nicolas, at the entry of the Vieux Port, with the guns facing inland to keep the citizens in order.

A short way down the right quay (as you look out to sea) is the elegant 17th-century Hôtel de Ville (Town Hall). Just behind, in rue de la Prison, is the Maison Diamantée, a 16th-century mansion with an elaborate interior staircase. The mansion now houses the **Musée du Vieux Marseille,** whose displays of costumes, pictures, and figurines depict old Marseille. *Rue de la Prison, tel. 91–55–10–19. Admission: 10 frs. adults, 5 frs. students and senior citizens, children free. Open Tues.–Sun. 10–5.*

㊶ Marseille's pompous, striped neo-Byzantine **cathedral** stands around the corner, but it is of considerably less interest than
㊷ the **Basilique St-Victor** across the water, in the shadow of the
㊸ **Fort St-Nicolas** (which can't be visited). With its powerful tower and thick-set walls, the basilica resembles a fortress and boasts one of southern France's oldest doorways (circa 1140), a 13th-

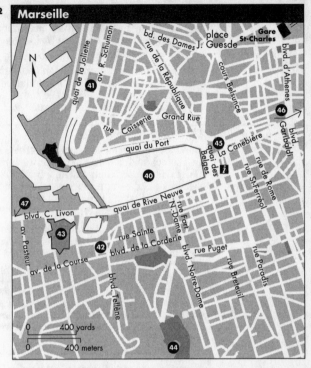

century nave, and a 14th-century chancel and transept. Downstairs, you'll find the murky 5th-century underground crypt, with its collection of ancient sarcophagi. *Rue Sainte.*

Time Out Just up the street from the basilica is the **Four des Navettes**—a bakery that has been producing slender, orange-spiced, shuttle-shaped *navette* loaves for over 200 years. Since the navettes can last for up to a year, they make good take-home presents, as well as on-the-spot snacks. *136 rue Sainte.*

A brisk half-mile walk up boulevard Tellène, followed by a trudge up a steep flight of steps, will take you to the foot of **Notre-Dame de la Garde.** This church, a flashy 19th-century cousin of the Sacré-Coeur in Paris and Fourvière in Lyon, features a similar hilltop location. The expansive view, clearest in early morning (especially if the mistral is blowing), stretches from the hinterland mountains to the sea via the Cité Radieuse, a controversial '50s housing project by Swiss-born architect Le Corbusier. The church's interior is generously endowed with bombastic murals, mosaics, and marble, while, at the top of the tower, the great gilded statue of the Virgin stands sentinel over the old port, 500 feet below. *Blvd. A. Aune.*

Return to the Vieux Port and venture along the legendary **La Canebière**—the "Can O' Beer" to prewar sailors—where stately mansions recall faded glory. La Canebière has been on the decline in recent years, but cafés and restaurants continue to provide an upbeat pulse. A hundred yards down on the left is the big white Palais de la Bourse (stock exchange) and, inside,

45 the **Musée de la Marine** (Nautical Museum), with a rundown on the history of the port and an interesting display of model ships. *Admission: 10 frs. Open Wed.–Mon. 9–noon and 2–6.*

Behind the bourse is the **Jardin des Vestiges,** a public garden that holds the remains of Roman foundations. Here you will find the little **Musée de l'Histoire de Marseille** (Town Museum), featuring exhibits related to the town's history. One of the highlights is the 60-foot Roman boat. *1 blvd. Philippon, tel. 91–62–30–78. Admission: 10 frs. adults, 5 frs. senior citizens and children. Open Tues.–Sat. 10–4:45.*

Continue past such busy shopping streets as rue Paradis, rue St-Ferréol, and rue de Rome, and turn right into boulevard Garibaldi to reach **cours Julien,** a traffic-free street lined with sidewalk cafés, restaurants, bookshops, and boutiques. The atmosphere is that of a scaled-down St-Germain-des-Prés wafted from Paris to the Mediterranean.

Return to La Canebière and, when you reach the undistinguished church of St-Vincent de Paul, fork left along cours Jeanne-Thierry (which becomes boulevard Longchamp) to the imposing **Palais Longchamp,** built in 1860 by the same architect who built Notre-Dame de la Garde, Henri Espérandieu (1829–
46 74). The palais is home to the **Musée des Beaux-Arts** (Fine Arts Museum); its collection of paintings and sculptures includes works by 18th-century Italian artist Giovanni Battista Tiepolo, Rubens, and French caricaturist and painter Honoré Daumier. *Tel. 91–62–21–17. Admission: 10 frs. adults, 5 frs. students and senior citizens. Open Tues.–Sun. 10–5.*

Marseille is no seaside resort, but a scenic 5-kilometer (3-mile) coast road (corniche du Président-J.-F.-Kennedy) links the Vieux-Port to the newly created Prado beaches in the swanky parts of southern Marseille. There are breathtaking views across the sea toward the rocky Frioul Islands, which can be visited by boat. Ninety-minute trips leave the Vieux-Port
47 hourly in summer and frequently in winter to visit the **Château d'If,** a castle in which various political prisoners were held captive down the ages. Alexandre Dumas condemned his fictional hero, the count of Monte Cristo, to be shut up in a cell here, before the wily count made his celebrated escape through a hole in the wall. *Admission included in the boat fare (40 frs.). Open June–Sept., daily 8:30–noon and 1:30–6:30; Oct.–May, daily 8:30–noon and 1:30–4.*

Numbers in the margin correspond to points of interest on the Provence map.

48 Head east from Marseille along D2 to **Aubagne,** 16 kilometers (10 miles) away. The headquarters of the French Foreign Legion is situated along D44A (turn left off D2 just before you reach Aubagne). The legion was created in 1831 and accepts recruits from all nations, no questions asked. The discipline and camaraderie instilled among its motley team of adventurers, criminals, and mercenaries has helped the legion forge a reputation for exceptional valor—a reputation romanticized by songs and films in which sweaty deeds of heroism are performed under the desert sun. The **Musée du Képi Blanc,** named after the *légionnaires'* distinctive white caps, does its best to polish the image by way of medals, uniforms, weapons, and photographs. *Caserne Viénot. Admission free. Open June–*

Sept., Tues.–Sun. 9–noon and 2–5; Oct.–May, Wed. and week-ends only, 9–noon.

Head south from Aubagne via D559/D1 to the fishing village of **Cassis**, 11 kilometers (7 miles) away. Cafés, restaurants, and seafood shops cluster around its harbor and three beaches, at the foot of Europe's highest cliff, the 1,300-foot Cap Canaille. Boats leave the harbor from quai St-Pierre to visit the neigh-boring *calanques*—long creeks that weave their way between towering white-stone cliffs. The farthest of the three calanques visited by boat, **En-Vau,** is the most intimidating; you may want to walk back from here along the scenic footpath.

From Cassis, a daring clifftop road runs along the top of Cap Canaille to the shipbuilding base of La Ciotat, 13 kilometers (8 miles) away. Stay on D559 for another 19 kilometers (12 miles), through Bandol, to **Sanary**, whose old streets and charming sea-front invite discovery. At neighboring Six-Fours-les-Plages, spin right on D616, around the Cap Sicié peninsula, in search of more fine panoramas and a colossal view across the Bay of Tou-lon.

Toulon is France's leading Mediterranean naval base. Leave your car in the underground parking lot at place de la Liberté, head along boulevard de Strasbourg, and turn right after the theater into rue Berthelot. This street leads into the pedestri-an streets that constitute the heart of old Toulon. Shops and colorful stalls make it an attractive area by day, but avoid it at night.

Time Out Good-value menus and a cozy setting make **La Ferme,** situated on a small square at the harbor end of cours Lafayette, a sensi-ble choice for a filling lunch. *6 pl. Louis-Blanc. Closed Sun. and Aug.*

Avenue de la République, an ugly array of concrete apartment blocks, runs parallel to the waterfront, where yachts and pleas-ure boats—some available for trips to the Iles d'Hyères or around the bay—add bright splashes of color. At the western edge of the quay is the **Musée Naval,** with large models of old and new ships, figureheads, paintings, and other items related to Toulon's maritime history. *Pl. Monsenergue. Admission: 20 frs. adults, 10 frs. children. Open Wed.–Mon. 9–noon and 2–5; closed Tues.*

Leading up from the quayside is the Cours Lafayette; on week-days it turns into a colorful street market selling glistening fish and masses of fruit.

Mighty hills surround Toulon. **Mont-Faron,** towering 1,600 feet above sea level, is the highest of all; its steep slopes veer up just outside the town. You can drive to the top, taking the circular route du Faron in either direction, or make the six-minute ascent by cable car from boulevard de l'Amiral Jean-Vence (operates 9:15–noon and 2:15–6, closed Mon., Sept.–May; call 94–92–68–25 to check operating times in winter or bad weather).

Head east from Toulon along D559 to Hyères-Plage, then turn right along D97 to **La Tour-Fondue** at the tip of the narrow Giens peninsula. Boats leave here frequently (every half hour in July and August) for the nearby island of Porquerolles. *Crossing time 20 min.; round-trip fare 70 frs.*

53 At five miles long, **Ile de Porquerolles** is the largest of the Iles d'Hyères, an archipelago spanning some 20 miles. Although the village of Porquerolles has several small hotels and restaurants, the main reason for coming here is simply to escape from the hustle of the modern world. Filmmakers love the island and use it as a handy base for shooting tropical or South Sea Island–type scenery. You can stroll across the island from the harbor to the lighthouse *(le phare)* in about 90 minutes, or head east among luxuriant flowers and thick woods.

Boats for two of the other islands in the archipelago leave from Hyères-Plages and, farther around the coast, from Port-de-
54 Miramar and Le Lavandou. The smaller of the two, **Ile de Port-Cros,** is classed as a national park and offers delightful,
55 well-marked nature trails. The **Ile du Levant** is long and rocky and much less interesting; the French navy has grabbed part of it, and much of the rest is occupied by the Heliopolis nudist camp.

What to See and Do with Children

The Wild West has invaded Provence at the **O.K. Corral,** a huge amusement park that piles on the thrills by way of roller coasters, Ferris wheels, and rootin' tootin' cowboy shows. Roy Rogers might do a double take at the less-than-authentic flavor—more Gallic than "Gunsmoke"—but children love it nonetheless. *11 km (7 mi) west of Aubagne on N8, just beyond Cuges-les-Pins, tel. 42–73–80–05. Admission: 70 frs. adults, 60 frs. children. Open June, daily 10:30–6:30; July–Aug., daily 10:30–7:30; Apr.–May and Sept., weekends 10:30–6:30; Mar. and Oct., Sun. 10:30–6:30.*

Just outside Stes-Maires-de-la-Mer is the **Musée de Cire** (also known as the **Musée du Boumian),** which provides an entertaining overview of local life by way of 18 scenes composed of waxwork figures. *Quartier Boumian, tel. 90–97–82–65. Admission: 25 frs. adults, 15 frs. children. Open Apr.–Oct., daily 10–noon and 2–7; Nov.–Mar., Sun. 10–noon and 2–6.*

The following attractions are covered in the Exploring text:

Boat tour of the calanques by Cassis, *see* Tour 3
Cathédrale d'Images, near Les Baux-de-Provence,
see Tour 1

Moulin de Daudet, Fontvieille, *see* Tour 1

Museon Arlaten, Arles, *see* Tour 1

Parc Ornithologique, north of Stes-Maries-de-la-Mer,
see Tour 1

Children may also enjoy the raucous flavor of the Marseille fish market, *see* Tour 3 (*see also* Shopping, *below*).

Off the Beaten Track

Our exploring tour bypasses Six-Fours-les-Plages on its way from the pretty harbor of Sanary to the dramatic Cap Scié peninsula. While Six-Fours is a sprawling town of limited interest, three nearby sites deserve a visit. The first is at Six-Fours itself, or, really, above it. The **Fort of Six-Fours,** at the top of a steep hill that has seemed even more rugged since fire destroyed its pine forest in 1987, can be seen for miles around. Although the fort is a private military base that can't be visited, the views across the Bay of Toulon are stupendous. Nearby is the former parish church of **St-Pierre,** featuring a Romanesque nave and a rich medieval altarpiece by Louis Bréa. Archaeological finds to the right of the entrance have revealed Roman walls built on the site.

Just north of Six-Fours (take D63 and turn left following signs marked *Monument Historique)* is the small stone chapel of **Notre-Dame de Pépiole,** hemmed in by pines and cypresses. While the chapel doesn't seem particularly interesting from a distance, it is, in fact, one of the oldest Christian buildings in France, dating from the 5th century. The simple interior has survived the years in remarkably good shape, although the colorful stained glass that fills the tiny windows is modern—composed mainly of broken bottles! *Chapel open most afternoons.*

Continue 5 kilometers (3 miles) north (via D11) to Ollioules and take N8 (direction Le Beausset) through the spectacular **Gorge d'Ollioules;** the 3-mile route twists its scenic way beneath awesome chalky rock faces. Turn right along D462 to pay a visit to the village of **Evenos,** a patchwork of inhabited and ruined houses dominated by an abandoned cliff-top castle.

Shopping

Gift Ideas *Santons,* colorful painted clay figures traditionally placed around a Christmas crib, make excellent gifts or souvenirs. There are literally hundreds of characters from which to choose, ranging from Mary, Joseph, and the Wise Men to fictional characters and notable personalities, both historic and contemporary. While santons can be found throughout the region (especially at Aubagne), the best places to purchase them are **Paul Fouque** (65 cours Gambetta, Aix-en-Provence) or **Atelier Ferriol** (2 chemin de Barriol, Arles).

Two specialties of Aix-en-Provence are deliciously fragrant soaps with natural floral scents and *calissons d'Aix,* ingeniously sculpted high-quality marzipan made of almonds and eggs. At **La Provence Gourmande** (66 rue Boulagon) you'll find a vast selection of soaps, as well as herbs, spices, and calissons d'Aix, while **À La Reine Jeanne** (32 cours Mirabeau) specializes in marzipan. Delicately patterned Provençal print fabrics made by Souleiado are beautiful and can be bought in lengths or already fashioned into dresses, scarves, tea cosies, and other accessories. You can find the prints in better-quality shops throughout the region, though Arles and Aix-en-Provence seem to have cornered most of the market.

Markets **Aix-en-Provence** has several markets that are a delight to explore: the flower market on Tuesday, Thursday, and Saturday mornings at place de l'Hôtel-de-Ville; the fruit and vegetable market every morning at place Richelme; and the fruit, vegetable, and herb market on Tuesday, Thursday, and Saturday mornings at place des Prêcheurs. There is also an antiques market on Tuesday, Thursday, and Saturday mornings at place de Verdun. At **Arles,** fruit, vegetables, and household goods are sold on Wednesday and Saturday mornings in the boulevard de Lices, while **Marseille's** famous fish market is held on Monday through Saturday mornings at the Vieux Port. The flower market at **Nîmes** is open Monday mornings at boulevard J-Jaurès, and you can purchase fruit, herbs, honey, and truffles at **Orange** on Thursday mornings in cours Aristide-Briand. Finally, in **Toulon,** there's a celebrated fish, fruit, and household-goods market from Monday to Saturday mornings on rue LaFayette near the harbor.

Sports and Fitness

Biking Bikes can be rented from train stations at Aix-en-Provence, Arles, Avignon, Marseille, Montpellier, Nîmes, and Orange; the cost is about 40 francs per day. Contact the **Comité Départemental de la Fédération Française de Cyclo** (2 rue Lavoisier, Avignon) for a list of the area's more scenic bike paths.

Bullfighting Provence's most popular spectator sport is bullfighting, both Spanish-style or the kinder *courses libres,* where the bulls have star billing and are often regarded as local heroes (they always live to fight another day). There are Spanish-style spectacles in the Roman arenas at Rond-Point des Arènes in **Arles** and at place des Arènes in **Nîmes.** Courses libres are also held at Nîmes and in nearly all the surrounding little villages throughout the summer.

Golf Golf is still considered a pastime for the rich, and you will find many more golf courses on the Riviera. However, Provence has an excellent course at La Grande Motte (tel. 67–56–05–00) and another near Aix-en-Provence (**Golf International du Château de l'Arc,** Rousset, tel. 42–53–28–38). Eighteen kilometers (11 miles) east of Hyéres is **Golf de Valcros** (Valcros, La Londe, tel. 94–66–81–02).

Hiking This has become newly popular in France, and you'll find blazed trails (discreet paint marks on rocks) on the best routes. Contact the **Comité Départemental** (63 av. C-Franck, Avignon) for a detailed list of trails and outfitters.

Horseback Riding Practically every locality in Provence has stables where horses can be rented. **Cheval Nomade** (col du Pointu, Bonnieux, tel. 90–74–40–48) specializes in tours on horseback (also, *see* Guided Tours under Essential Information, *above*). In Avignon, **Barthelasse** (Chemin du Mont Blanc, tel. 90–85–83–48) offers lessons for children at **Le Pony Club,** a children's riding school, in addition to renting horses to more experienced equestrians.

Water Sports You can windsurf and sail at La Grande Motte, Stes-Maries-de-la-Mer, Carry-le Rouet and Martigues (near Marseille), Cassis, Hyères-Plage, and the island of Porquerolles, where equipment and sailboats can be rented. In Hyères, the **Wanako School of Windsurf and Sunboards** (5 Centre de Nautisme, tel. 94–57–77–20) rents sailboats starting at 300 francs for the day, while a windsurfer starts at 320 francs.

Dining and Lodging

Dining

Provence has more than its share of France's top restaurants. Thank tourism for this: Nature didn't intend for Provence to be a gastronomic paradise. There are no deep, damp pastures for cattle and no chill rivers for salmon. In the old days, cooking was based on olive oil, fruit, and vegetables grown in valleys where summer irrigation is possible; salt cod was another staple, while the heady scent and flavor of garlic and wild herbs from stony, sunbaked hills improved the scant meat dishes. The current gastronomic scene is a far cry from this frugality: Wealthy tourists demand caviar and champagne, and Parisian chefs have created internationally renowned restaurants to satisfy them. Still, there's a lot to be said for simple Provençal food on a vine-shaded terrace. Have a *pastis*, that pale green, anise-based aperitif, accompanied by black olives, or try the *tapenade*, a delicious paste of capers, anchovies, olives, oil, and lemon juice, best smeared on chunks of garlic-rubbed bread. Follow it up with *crudités* (raw vegetables served with *aïoli*, a garlicky mayonnaise) and a simple dish of grilled lamb or beef, accompanied by a bottle of chilled rosé. Locals like to end their meal with a round of goat cheese and fruit.

The Provençal image comes through in a love of color; bell peppers, eggplant, zucchini, saffron, and tomatoes crop up everywhere. Fish is very trendy these days. A trip to the fish market at Marseille will reveal the astronomical price of the fresh local catch; in the Mediterranean there are too few fish chased by too many boats. Steer clear of the multitude of cheap Marseille fish restaurants, many with brisk ladies out front who deliver throaty sales pitches; any inexpensive fish menu must use frozen imports. The Marseille specialty of *bouillabaisse* is a case in point: Once a fisherman's cheap stew of spanking-fresh specimens too small or bony to put on sale, it has now become a celebration dish, with such heretical additions as lobster. The high-priced versions can be delicious, but avoid the cheaper ones, undoubtedly concocted with canned, frozen, and even powdered ingredients.

Highly recommended restaurants are indicated by a star ★.

Category	Cost*
Very Expensive	over 400 francs
Expensive	250–400 francs
Moderate	125–250 francs
Inexpensive	under 125 francs

*per person for a three-course meal, including tax (18.6%) and tip but not wine

Lodging

Accommodations are varied in this much-visited part of France and range from luxurious *mas* (converted farmhouses) to modest downtown hotels convenient for sightseeing. Service is often less than prompt, a casualty of the sweltering summer heat. Reservations are essential for much of the year, and many hotels are closed during winter.

Highly recommended hotels are indicated by a star ★.

Category	Cost*
Very Expensive	over 800 francs
Expensive	400–800 francs
Moderate	200–400 francs
Inexpensive	under 200 francs

All prices are for a standard double room for two, including tax (18.6%) and service charge.

Aix-en-Provence
Dining
★

Le Clos de la Violette. Aix's best restaurant lies in a residential district north of the old town. You can eat under the chestnut trees or in the charming, airy dining room. Chef Jean-Marc Banzo uses only fresh, local ingredients in his nouvelle and traditional recipes. Try the *saumon vapeur*, an aromatic steamed salmon. The weekday lunch menu is moderately priced and well worth the trek uptown. *10 av. de la Violette, tel. 42–23–30–71. Reservations advised. Jacket required. AE, MC, V. Closed Sun., Mon. lunch, early Nov., and most of Mar. Expensive.*

Brasserie Royale. This noisy, bustling eatery on cours Mirabeau serves up hearty Provençal dishes amid a background din of banging pots, vociferous waiters, and tumultuous cries for more wine. The best place to eat is in the glassed-in patio out front, so you can soak up the Champs-Elysées-style atmosphere of the leafy boulevard while enjoying your meal. *17 cours Mirabeau, tel. 42–26–01–63. Reservations advised. Dress: casual. AE, V. Inexpensive.*

Lodging
★

Mercure-Paul Cézanne. Jean-Claude Tresy runs this stately town-house hotel, and his taste for antiques and ornate furnishings has made it a civilized and sophisticated place. Each guest room is individually decorated with lots of marble, gilt, and period furniture. There's no restaurant. *40 av. Victor-Hugo, 13100, tel. 42–26–34–73. 56 rooms with bath. AE, DC, MC, V. Expensive.*

Nègre-Coste. A cours Mirabeau location makes this hotel both a convenient and an atmospheric choice; it's extremely popular, so make reservations long in advance. The elegant 18th-century town house has been completely modernized but features a luxurious Old World decor that extends to the guest rooms as well as the public areas. The views from the front rooms are worth the extra bit of noise. There's no restaurant. *33 cours Mirabeau, 13100, tel. 42–27–74–22. 37 rooms with bath. AE, DC, MC, V. Moderate–Expensive.*

Anduze
Dining and Lodging

Le Ranquet. A hilly, wooded setting; an outdoor pool; a piano bar; and 10 stylish, spacious, air-conditioned rooms justify the 32-kilometer (20-mile) detour to Le Ranquet, northwest of Nîmes. Annie Majourel is one of France's few top-ranking female chefs; her menus (two are moderately priced) change every two months. *Rte. de St-Hippolyte du Fort, Tornac, 30140 Anduze, tel. 66–77–51–63. 10 rooms with bath. Facilities: restaurant, piano bar, pool. MC, V. Closed Tues. and Wed. out of season, mid-Nov.–Christmas, and Feb. Expensive.*

Arles
Dining

Le Vaccarès. In an upstairs restaurant overlooking place du Forum, chef Bernard Dumas serves classical Provençal dishes with a touch of invention and some particularly good seafood creations. Try his mussels dressed in herbs and garlic. The dining-room decor is as elegant as the cuisine. *11 rue Favorin, tel. 90–96–06–17. Reservations advised. Dress: casual. MC, V.*

Closed end of Dec.–end of Jan., Sun. dinner, and Mon. Moderate–Expensive.

Lodging **Arlatan.** Follow the signposts from place du Forum to the picturesque street where you'll find this 15th-century house, former home of the counts of Arlatan and built on the site of a 4th-century basilica (tiled flooring dating from this period is visible below glass casing). The hotel was renovated in 1989, and antiques, pretty fabrics, and lots of tapestries and elegant furniture lend it a gracious atmosphere. There's no restaurant, but there is an attractive garden and a private bar. *26 rue du Sauvage, 13200, tel. 90–93–56–66. 51 rooms with bath. Facilities: garden. AE, DC, MC, V. Expensive.*

Dining and Lodging **Jules César.** This elegant hotel was originally a Carmelite convent, and many guest rooms overlook the attractive 17th-century cloisters. The rooms are tastefully decorated with antiques, and the garden is an oasis of tranquillity. The restaurant, Lou Marquès, is the most fashionable eating place in Arles, thanks to new chef Pascal Renaud, who pleases his international clientele with both nouvelle cuisine and traditional Provençal dishes. Try his cod with lentils and fresh cream. *Blvd. des Lices, 13200, tel. 90–93–43–20. 55 rooms with bath. Facilities: restaurant, garden, pool. AE, DC, MC, V. Closed Nov.–Dec. 23. Expensive.*

★ **Mas de la Chapelle.** A 16th-century farmhouse surrounded by pretty gardens and outbuildings is the setting of this fine hotel-restaurant, reader-recommended for an overnight stay or to use as a base from which to explore the area. It features an ancient chapel that has been skillfully converted into a cozy—though sometimes stifling—restaurant, decorated with Aubusson tapestries and original 18th-century stained glass. The menu varies; the seasonal game dishes are a good bet, or try the *coquilles St.-Jacques.* There is one slight drawback, however: the nearby whoosh of high-speed trains. *Petite Route de Tarascon, 13200, tel. 90–93–23–15. 13 rooms with bath. Facilities: restaurant, riding, tennis, pool, park. AE, DC, MC, V. Closed Feb. Moderate–Expensive.*

Avignon **Hiély-Lucullus.** According to most authorities, this establishment numbers among the top-50 restaurants in France, although André Chaussy has now taken over as chef for the legendary Pierre Hiély. The upstairs dining room has a quiet, dignified charm and is run with aplomb by Madame Hiély. Traditional delicacies include crayfish tails in scrambled eggs hidden inside a puff-pastry case. Save room for the extensive cheese board. *5 rue de la République, tel. 90–86–17–07. Reservations required. Dress: neat but casual. AE, V. Closed most of Jan., last 2 weeks in June, Mon. and Tues. lunch. Moderate–Expensive.*

Dining
★

Dining and Lodging **Les Frênes.** The thumbnail-size town of Montfavet, 5 kilometers (3 miles) outside Avignon, is the setting for this luxurious hotel-restaurant. The country house features gardens to ramble in, splashing fountains, and individually decorated guest rooms; the styles range from subtle modern to art deco. Whatever the period of decor, each room is distinctive and equipped with every modern convenience. The excellent restaurant specializes in stylish country cuisine; the pigeon with black truffles in a puff-pastry case is always a good bet. *645 av. des Vertes-Rives, 84140 Montfavet, tel. 90–31–17–93. 15 rooms with bath. Facilities: garden, pool, restaurant, tennis, sauna,* *golf. AE, DC, MC, V. Closed Nov.–early Mar. Very Expensive.*

Europe. This noble 16th-century town house became a hotel in Napoleonic times. In fact, the great man himself was one of the very first customers; since then, everyone from crowned heads of state to Robert and Elizabeth Browning has stayed here. Lovers of gracious living find it an excellent value; the guest rooms are spacious, filled with period furniture, and feature lavishly appointed modern bathrooms. Make reservations well in advance. The restaurant, La Vieille Fontaine, features respectable regional cuisine, and you can eat outside in the stone courtyard. Gourmands will want to try the chicken with wild mushrooms or the duck liver. *12 pl. Crillon, 84000, tel. 90–82–66–92. 50 rooms with bath. Facilities: restaurant. AE, DC, MC, V. Restaurant Closed Sat. lunch and Sun. Expensive.*

Les Baux-de-Provence
Dining and Lodging
★

L'Oustaù de Baumanière. An idyllic setting under chalky-white cliffs, sumptuous guest rooms, and exquisite food make this a place of pilgrimage for lovers of the good life. The top-ranking restaurant occupies an old Provençal farmhouse; you'll be served your meal in a cavernous room decked out with ornate furniture and resembling a luxurious crypt. Try a plump pigeon stuffed with foie gras or some simple local thyme-fed lamb. The guest rooms are fit for a monarch—Queen Elizabeth II has slept here. *Le Vallon, 13520 Les Baux-de-Provence, tel. 90–54–33–07. 25 rooms with bath. Facilities: restaurant, tennis, pool, riding. Restaurant reservations required. AE, DC, MC, V. Closed late Jan.–early Mar.; restaurant closed Wed., Thurs. lunch Sept.–June. Very Expensive.*

Gordes
Dining

Comptoir du Victuailler. You'll find only 10 tables at this tiny restaurant in the village center, which serves elegantly simple meals using only the freshest local ingredients: capon, guinea fowl, asparagus, artichokes, truffles. . . . The fruit sorbets are a revelation, and there is an admirable choice of little-known Rhône wines. *Place du Château, tel. 90–72–01–31. Reservations required. Dress: neat but casual. MC, V. Closed mid-Nov.–mid-Dec., mid-Jan.–mid-Mar., Tues. dinner, and Wed. Sept.–May. Expensive.*

Dining and Lodging

Domaine de l'Enclos. Small, private stone cottages make up this charming hotel just outside Gordes; they have deceptively simple exteriors, but inside you'll find them luxurious in a quaint, countrified way. The restaurant serves remarkably good nouvelle dishes; the menu varies with the seasons, but if it's offered, try the excellent aromatic duck. *Rte. de Sénanque, 84220 Gordes, tel. 90–72–08–22. 14 rooms with bath. Facilities: restaurant, pool, tennis. AE, MC, V. Expensive.*

Ile de Porquerolles
Dining and Lodging
★

Mas du Langoustier. This luxurious hideout lies amid some stunningly lush terrain at the westernmost point of the island, 3 kilometers (2 miles) from the harbor. Anchor your yacht, and Madame Richard will pick you up in a handy launch; arrive by ferry, and she'll send a car to meet you. The rooms are delightful, the views superb. Hotel guests must eat their meals here (no hardship), but the restaurant is open to nonresidents, too. Chef Michel Sarran uses a delicate nouvelle touch with his seafood dishes; try the fresh sardines in ginger or the grilled red mullet or lobster. *83400 Ile de Porquerolles, tel. 94–58–30–09. 60 rooms with bath. Facilities: restaurant, tennis, private beach. AE, DC, MC, V. Closed mid-Nov.–mid-Mar. Expensive.*

Marseille
Dining
★

Chez Fonfon. The Marseillais come here for the best bouillabaisse in the world, and past diners lured by the top-quality seafood have included John Wayne and Nikita Khrushchev. "Fonfon" is the chef, sometimes known as Alphonse Mounier; he's thinking of retiring, but a successor is being trained to his rigorous standards. The restaurant is located on the corniche J. F. Kennedy, which twists its scenic path around the edges of the Mediterranean; the great sea views come gratis. *140 rue du Vallon des Auffes, tel. 91–52–14–38. Reservations strongly advised. Jacket and tie advised. AE, DC, MC, V. Closed Oct., Christmas–New Year's, Sat. and Sun. Expensive.*

Chez Madie. Every morning Madie Minassian, the colorful *patronne*, bustles along the quayside to trade insults with the fishwives at the far end of the Vieux Port—and scour their catch for the freshest ingredients, which swiftly end up in her bouillabaisse, fish soup, *favouilles* sauce (made with tiny local crabs), and other dishes you'll savor from the good-value menus at her restaurant. *138 quai du Port, tel. 91–90–40–87. Reservations advised. Dress: casual. AE, DC, MC, V. Closed Mon., Sun. dinner, and most of Aug. Moderate.*

Dar Djerba. This is perhaps the best of the North African restaurants that are scattered throughout Marseille. The cozy, white-walled Dar Djerba on bustling cours Julien specializes in couscous of all kinds (with lamb, chicken, or even quail) as well as Arab coffees and pastries. The Moorish tile patterns and exotic aromas will waft you away on a Saharan breeze. *15 cours Julien, tel. 91–48–55–36. Reservations advised in summer. Dress: casual. DC, MC, V. Closed Tues. and second half of Aug. Moderate.*

Dining and Lodging
★

Sofitel. The Sofitel possesses more appeal than most modern chain hotels, mainly because of the idyllic views across the old fort to the Vieux Port. Rooms with a balcony are more expensive, but the pleasure of an outdoor breakfast in the morning sunshine—possible most of the year—is worth a splurge. The top-floor restaurant, Les Trois Forts, boasts stunning panoramic views and delicious Provençal fare; the red mullet, flavored with pepper, is superb. *36 blvd. Charles-Livon, 13007, tel. 91–52–90–19. 127 rooms with bath. Facilities: pool, restaurant. AE, DC, MC, V. Very Expensive.*

Lodging
★

Pullman Beauvau. Right on the Vieux Port, a few steps from the end of La Canebière, the Beauvau is the ideal town hotel. The 200-year-old former coaching inn was totally modernized in 1986, and its charming Old World opulence is enhanced by wood paneling, designer fabrics, fine paintings, genuine antique furniture—and exceptional service. The best rooms look out onto the Vieux Port. There's no restaurant, but you can start your day in the cozy breakfast room. *4 rue Beauvau, 13001, tel. 91–54–91–00 (to make reservations toll-free from the U.S., call 800/223–9868; in the U.K., 071/621–1962). 71 rooms with bath. Facilities: bar, breakfast room. AE, DC, MC, V. Expensive.*

Lutétia. There's nothing remarkable about this small hotel, but its rooms are quiet, airy, modernized, and a good value for the money, given the handy setting between La Canebière and St-Charles rail station. *38 allée Léon-Gambetta, 13001, tel. 91–50–81–78. 29 rooms with bath or shower. DC, MC, V. Moderate.*

Montpellier **Le Chandelier.** The only complaints here concern the prices à la
Dining carte; the service is impeccable, the trendy pink decor is more
than acceptable, and the inventive cuisine is delicious. Try the
lobster in lasagne or the pigeon. There's a sound wine list, and
the cinnamon-honey ice cream makes a fine end to your meal.
*3 rue Leenhardt, tel. 67–92–61–62. Reservations advised.
Dress: casual. AE, DC, MC, V. Closed part of Feb., first 2
weeks in Aug., Sun., and Mon. lunch. Moderate–Expensive.*
Petit Jardin. As the name implies, you can dine here in a charming leafy garden, within sight of the cathedral; the cheerful,
flower-bedecked dining room is equally pleasant. Owner Ro-
land Heilmann has made a rapid name for himself with such
tasty regional dishes as *bourride* (fish soup made with monk- or
anglerfish) and the *piperade* omelet with king-size prawns. *20
rue Jean-Jacques Rousseau, tel. 67–60–78–78. Reservations
advised. Dress: casual. AE, DC, MC, V. Closed Sun. evening,
Mon., and Jan.–Mar. Moderate.*

Nîmes **Nicolas.** Locals have long known about this homey place, which
Dining is always packed; you'll hear the noise before you open the door.
★ A friendly, frazzled staff serves up delicious *bourride* (a garlicky fish soup) and other local specialties—all at unbelievably
low prices. *1 rue Poise, tel. 66–67–50–47. Reservations strongly advised. Dress: casual. MC, V. Closed Mon., first 2 weeks in
July, and mid-Dec.–first week in Jan. Inexpensive.*

Dining and Lodging **Impérator.** This little palace-hotel, just a few minutes' walk
★ from the Jardin de La Fontaine, has been totally modernized in
excellent taste. Most guest rooms retain a quaint Provençal
feel, and all are cozy but spacious. If this hotel were suddenly
whisked to the Riviera, you would expect to pay twice as much
for the pleasure of staying here. The fine restaurant, L'Enclos
de la Fontaine, is Nîmes's most fashionable eating place, where
chef Jean-Michel Nigon provides such inventive dishes as iced,
dill-perfumed *langoustine* (crayfish) soup, and calves' liver
with blackcurrant sauce and Calvados-soaked apples. The
moderately priced set menus are bargains, but you can easily
order your way into the expensive level. *15 rue Gaston-
Boissier, 30000, tel. 66–21–90–30. 59 rooms with bath. Facilities: restaurant. AE, DC, MC, V. Restaurant closed Sat.
lunch. Moderate–Expensive.*
Louvre. Occupying a 17th-century house on a leafy square near
the Roman arena, the Louvre is the best sort of carefully run
provincial hotel. The guest rooms are spacious and have high
ceilings, and they manage to retain the feel of a private house;
ask for one that faces the courtyard. The restaurant serves
well-prepared traditional cuisine. The most tempting dishes
are at the moderate level, though the inexpensive menu is a remarkably good deal. Seafood addicts will enjoy the lobster or
the mussels in a flaky pastry crust. *2 sq. de la Couronne, 30000,
tel. 66–67–22–75. 33 rooms with bath. Facilities: restaurant.
AE, DC, MC, V. Moderate.*

Orange **Le Pigraillet.** One of Orange's best lunch spots is Le Pigraillet,
Dining on the Chemin Colline St-Eutrope at the far end of the gardens.
★ You may want to eat in the garden, but most diners seek shelter
from the mistral in the glassed-in terrace. The modern cuisine
includes crab ravioli, foie gras in port, and duck breast in the
muscat wine of nearby Beaumes-de-Venise. *Colline St-
Eutrope, tel. 90–34–44–25. Reservations advised. Jacket*

required. MC, V. Closed Jan.–Feb. and Mon. Moderate–Expensive.

Le Bec Fin. While hardly elegant, Le Bec Fin is a perfect example of a small-town restaurant, serving local specialties to tourists and locals alike. Try the rabbit with mustard for a real taste of Provençal cooking at its best. *14 rue Segond-Wéber, tel. 90–34–14–76. Reservations accepted. Dress: casual. No credit cards. Closed Thurs., Fri., and Nov. Inexpensive.*

St-Rémy-de-Provence
Lodging

Château des Alpilles. This lavishly appointed, 19th-century château lords it over a fine park. In its heyday, it counted statesmen and aristocrats among its guests. The crowd these days is almost as sophisticated, and the guest rooms offer the best in classic luxury. Decorators have gone wild with plush carpeting and wood furniture to enhance the elegant ambience. Many rooms are equipped with kitchenettes. *Ancienne route du Grès, 13210 St-Rémy-de-Provence, tel. 90–92–03–33. 15 rooms with bath. AE, DC, MC, V. Facilities: pool, tennis, sauna, gardens. Closed Jan.–mid-Mar. Expensive.*

★ **Château de Roussan.** A manicured 15-acre park makes a lush setting for this 18th-century mansion, a mile outside town on the road to Tarascon. Originally a country retreat for the Roussan family, the château was converted into a hotel just after World War II. Today it seems so well preserved that it's almost spooky. The interior is quiet and gracious and appears virtually unaltered, save for the newly renovated bathrooms. The guest rooms are large and comfortable, and many feature pleasant parkland views. *Rte. de Tarascon, 13210 St-Rémy-de-Provence, tel. 90–92–11–63. 20 rooms with bath. Facilities: restaurant, park. AE, MC, V. Closed mid-Nov.–Christmas and Jan.–mid-Mar. Moderate–Expensive.*

The Arts and Nightlife

The Arts

Theater and Music

The summer music and drama festivals at Aix-en-Provence, Arles, Avignon, and Orange attract top performers. At Aix, the **International Arts and Music Festival**, with first-class opera, symphonic concerts, and chamber music, flourishes from mid-July to mid-August; its principal venue is the Théâtre de l'Archevêché in the courtyard of the Archbishop's Palace (pl. des Martyrs de la Résistance). At Arles, the **Music and Drama Festival** takes place in July in the Théâtre Antique (rue de la Calade/rue du Cloître). Avignon's prestigious **International Music and Drama Festival,** held during the last three weeks of July, is centered on the Grand Courtyard of the Palais des Papes (pl. du Palais, tel. 90–86–24–43). The **International Opera Festival** in Orange, during the last two weeks of July, takes place in the best-preserved Roman theater in existence, the Théâtre Antique (pl. des Frerès-Mounet).

Opera and concerts are performed throughout the year in Aix-en-Provence's 18th-century Théâtre Municipal (rue de l'Opéra, tel. 42–38–07–39), while Montpellier presents similar spectacles at the 19th-century Théâtre des Treize Vents (pl. de la Comédie, tel. 67–52–77–17).

Nightlife

Provence is a disappointing provincial backwater as far as razzle-dazzle nightlife goes; if you've come to the south of France hoping to paint the place red—keep heading east to the Riviera. Your best bets for clubs and discos are towns that have a major student population—such as Aix-en-Provence, Marseille, and Montpellier—or the seaside resorts of La Grande Motte and Stes-Maries-de-la-Mer. Most night spots open and close with alarming frequency, but at press time, Marseille's major cabaret-nightclub was still going strong: **Au Son des Guitares** (18 rue Corneille). Disco lovers should try the **London Club** (73 corniche-J.-F.-Kennedy). In Montpellier, we suggest **Le Rimmel** (4 bis rue de Boussairolles); in La Grande Motte, **Copacabana** (Grand Travers, rte. des Plages). Aix has a noteworthy jazz club, **Scat Club** (11 rue de la Verrerie), and Marseille has **Jazz Hot** (48 av. la Rose). Finally, for those who thrive on roulette and blackjack, go to **The Casino,** open from 3 PM to 2 AM (2 bis av. Napoléon-Bonaparte, Aix-en-Provence).

4 The Riviera

St-Tropez to Monaco

It's important to begin with a realistic sense of Riviera life so you won't spend your holiday nursing wounded expectations. The Riviera conjures up images of fabulous yachts and villas, movie stars and palaces, and budding starlets sunning themselves on ribbons of golden sand. The truth is that most beaches, at least east of Cannes, are small and pebbly. In summer, hordes of visitors are stuffed into concrete high rises or roadside campsites—on weekends it can take two hours to drive the last six miles into St-Tropez. Yes, the film stars are here—but in their private villas. When the merely wealthy come, they come off-season, in the spring and fall—the best time for you to visit, too.

That said, we can still recommend the Riviera, even in summer, as long as you're selective about the places you choose to visit. A few miles inland are fortified medieval towns perched on mountaintops, high above the sea. The light that Renoir and Matisse came to capture is as magical here as ever. Fields of roses and lavender still send their heady perfume up to these fortified towns, where craftspeople make and sell their wares, as their predecessors did in the Middle Ages. Some resorts are as exclusive as ever, and no one will argue that the chefs hereabouts have lost their touch.

It's impossible to be bored along the Riviera. You can try a different beach or restaurant every day. When you've had enough of the sun, you can visit pottery towns like Vallauris, where Picasso worked, or perfumeries at Grasse, where three-quarters of the world's essences are produced. You can drive along dizzying gorges, one almost as deep as the Grand Canyon. You can disco or gamble the night away in Monte Carlo and shop for the best Paris has to offer, right in Cannes or Nice. Only minutes from the beaches are some of the world's most famous museums of modern art, featuring the works of Fernand Léger, Henri Matisse, Pablo Picasso, Pierre-Auguste Renoir, Jean Cocteau—all the artists who were captivated by the light and color of the Côte d'Azur.

Essential Information

Important Addresses and Numbers

Tourist Information The Riviera's regional tourist office is the **Comité Régional du Tourisme de Riviera–Côte d'Azur** (55 promenade des Anglais, 06000 Nice; written inquiries only). Local tourist offices in major towns covered in this chapter are as follows: **Antibes** (11 pl. Général-de-Gaulle, tel. 93–33–95–64), **Cannes** (Palais des Festivals, 1 La Croisette, tel. 93–39–24–53), **Juan-les-Pins** (51 blvd. Guillaumont, tel. 93–61–04–98), **La Napoule** (272 av. Henri-Clews, tel. 93–49–95–31), **Menton** (Palais de l'Europe, av. Boyer, tel. 93–57–57–00), **Monte Carlo** (2-A blvd. des Moulins, tel. 93–30–87–01), **Nice** (av. Thiers, tel. 93–87–07–07), and **St-Tropez** (quai Jean-Jaurès, tel. 94–97–45–21).

Travel Agencies **American Express** (8 rue des Belges, Cannes, tel. 93–38–15–87; 11 promenade des Anglais, Nice, tel. 93–87–29–82; and 43 blvd. Albert-Ier, tel. 93–34–74–56) and **Wagons-Lits** (2 av. Monte-Carlo, Monte Carlo, tel. 93–25–01–05).

Car Rental **Avis** (9 av. d'Ostende, Monte Carlo, tel. 93–30–17–53; and av. du 8-Mai-1945, St-Tropez, tel. 94–97–03–10), **Europcar** (9 av.

Thiers, Menton, tel. 93–28–21–80), and **Hertz** (147 rue d'Antibes, Cannes, tel. 93–99–04–20; and 12 av. du Suede, Nice, tel. 93–87–11–87).

Arriving and Departing

By Plane The area's only international airport is at Nice; for information and reservations, call 93–21–30–12.

By Train Mainline trains from the French capital stop at most of the major resorts; the trip to Nice takes about seven hours.

By Car If you're traveling from Paris by car, you can avoid a lengthy drive by taking the overnight motorail *(train-auto-couchette)* service to Nice, which departs from Paris's Gare de Bercy, five minutes from the Gare de Lyon. Otherwise, leave Paris by A6 (becoming A7 after Lyon), which continues down to Avignon. Here A8 branches off east toward Italy, with convenient exit/entry points for all major towns (except St-Tropez).

Getting Around

By Train The train is a practical and inexpensive way of getting around the Riviera and stops at dozens of stations.

By Car If you prefer to avoid the slower, albeit spectacularly scenic, coastal roads, opt for the Italy-bound A8.

By Bus Local buses cover a network of routes along the Riviera and stop at many out-of-the-way places that can't be reached by train. Timetables are available from tourist offices, train stations, and the local bus depots *(gares routières)*.

Guided Tours

Bus Tours Two of the largest companies offering 1½-day tours are **Santa Azur** (11 av. Jean-Médecin, 06000 Nice, tel. 93–85–46–81) and **CTM** (Compagnie des Transports Méditerranéens, 5 sq. Mérimée, 06100 Cannes, tel. 93–39–07–68). CTM has a day trip to St-Tropez on Thursday (about 150 francs), as well as a half-day excursion to St-Raphäel and Lac de St-Cassien (about 100 francs); buses leave on Tuesday and Thursday at 8 AM. Santa Azur's one-day tour destinations include Nice (Monday, Wednesday, and Friday; 100 francs), Monaco, and the hill town of Eze (Monday, Wednesday, Friday, and Sunday; 120 francs).

Boat Tours **Gallus Excursions 80** (24 quai Lunel, 06000 Nice, tel. 93–55–33–33) offers an enjoyable day-long jaunt to the Iles de Lérins; the cost is about 150 francs.

Special-Interest Any tourist office will produce a sheaf of suggestions on gourmandizing, golfing, and walking tours, among others. **Novatour** (9 rue de Lille, 06400 Cannes, tel. 93–69–47–47) offers tailor-made packages for its clients, though museum tours are a specialty; a three-day/two-night museum tour of Vence and Antibes, including half-board, costs about 3,000 francs.

Exploring the Riviera

Numbers in the margin correspond to points of interest on the Riviera maps.

Orientation

Our Riviera text covers the 75 miles between St-Tropez and the Italian border. The first tour concentrates on the Mediterranean coast from St-Tropez to Cannes and Antibes. The second begins with the inland towns of Grasse, Vence, and St-Paul-de-Vence, then rejoins the Mediterranean at Cagnes and continues to Nice and Monaco.

Highlights for First-time Visitors

Sunning on the beach at St-Tropez, Tour 1
A stroll down La Croisette, Cannes, Tour 1
Picasso Museum in the Château Grimaldi, Antibes, Tour 1
A walk along the Cap d'Antibes peninsula, Tour 1
St-Paul-de-Vence, Tour 2
Fondation Maeght, La Gardette, Tour 2
Old Town, Nice, Tour 2
Musée Ephrussi de Rothschild, St-Jean-Cap-Ferrat, Tour 2
The hill village of Peillon, Tour 2
Casino at Monte Carlo, Tour 2

Tour 1. St-Tropez to Antibes

❶ Old money never came to **St-Tropez,** but Brigitte Bardot did. Bardot came with her director Roger Vadim in 1956 to film *And God Created Woman,* and the resort has never been the same. Actually, the village was first "discovered" by the writer Guy de Maupassant (1850–93) and again, later, by the French painter Paul Signac (1863–1935), who came in 1892 and brought his friends—Matisse, Pierre Bonnard, and others. What attracted them was the pure, radiant light and the serenity and colors of the landscape. The writer Colette moved into a villa here between the two world wars and contributed to its notoriety. When the movie people staked their claim in the 1950s, St-Tropez became St-Trop (*trop* in French means "too much").

Anything associated with the distant past almost seems absurd in St-Tropez. Still, the place has a history that predates the invention of the string bikini, and people have been finding reasons to come here for centuries. First, in AD 68 there was a Roman soldier from Pisa named Torpes who was beheaded for professing his Christian faith in the presence of the emperor Nero. The headless body was put in a boat between a dog and a cock and sent drifting out to sea. The body eventually floated ashore, perfectly preserved, still watched over by the two animals. The buried remains became a place of pilgrimage, which by the 4th century was called St-Tropez. In the late 15th century, under the Genovese, St-Tropez became a small independent republic.

Since then, people have come for the sun and the sea, and, starting in the 1950s, the celebrities. But whatever celebrities there are here stay hidden away in villas, and the people you'll see are mere mortals—lots of them. In summer, the population swells from 7,000 to 64,000 and the beaches are filled with every imaginable type of human animal, each displaying the best (or at least the most) of his or her youth, beauty, or wealth.

Off-season is the time to come, but even in summer there are reasons to stay. The soft, sandy beaches are the best on the coast. Take an early morning stroll along the harbor or down the narrow medieval streets—the rest of the town will still be sleeping off the Night Before—and you'll see just how pretty St-Tropez is, with its tiny squares and rich, pastel-colored houses bathed in light. There's a weekend's worth of trendy boutiques to explore—to be delighted or shocked by—and many cute cafés, where you can sit under colored awnings sipping wine and feel very French. Five minutes from town, you'll be in a green world of vineyards and fields, where you'll see nothing more lascivious than a butterfly fluttering around some chestnut leaves or a grapevine clinging to a farmhouse wall. Above the fertile fields are mountains crowned with medieval villages, where you can come at dusk for wildstrawberry tarts and fabulous views. Perhaps it's the soft light, perhaps the rich fields and faded pastels, but nowhere else along the coast will you experience so completely the magic of Provence.

Two cafés on the harbor provide dress-circle seats for admiring the St-Tropez scene: **Le Gorille,** on quai Suffren, and **Sénequier's,** the café with the big terrace on quai Jean-Juarès, beyond the tourist office. Walk along the harbor, filled with pleasure boats, and along the breakwater (the Môle), and continue to the **Musée de l'Annonciade,** a church converted into a major art museum. The collection of Impressionist paintings is filled with views of St-Tropez by Matisse, Bonnard, Paul Signac, Maurice de Vlaminck, and others. *Quai de l'Epi. Admission: 20 frs. adults, 10 frs. children. Open Wed.–Mon. 10–noon and 2–6; closed Tues.*

Rue de la Citadelle leads inland from the tourist office to the **Citadel,** a 16th-century fortress with commanding views from St-Tropez across the bay to Ste-Maxime. In the keep is the **Musée de la Marine,** stocked with marine paintings and ship models, including a Greek galley. *Admission: 18 frs. Open Nov.– Easter, Wed.–Mon. 10–5; Easter–Oct., 10–noon and 2–4:30; closed Tues.*

Stroll down Montée Ringrave to **place Carnot,** site of a twice-weekly market (Saturday/Tuesday) and daily games of *boules.* Trendy boutiques are on **rue Sibilli.**

Time Out Food at the **Café des Arts** may be ordinary, but the café is a popular place in which to sit and feel as if you're part of the in-crowd. *Pl. Carnot. Closed Oct.–Mar.*

Beaches close to town—**Plage des Greniers** and the **Bouillabaisse**—are great for families, but holiday people snub them, preferring a 6-mile sandy crescent at **Les Salins** and **Pampellone.** These beaches are about 3 kilometers (2 miles) from town, so it helps to have a car, motorbike, or bicycle.

2 Visitors seem to enjoy a trip through **Port-Grimaud,** a modern architect's idea of a Provençal fishing village-cum-Venice, built out into the gulf for the yachting crowd—each house with its own mooring. Particularly appealing are the harmonious pastel colors, which have weathered nicely, and the graceful bridges over the canals.

3 From St-Tropez, take D93 south 11 kilometers (7 miles) to the old Provençal market town of **Ramatuelle.** The ancient houses are huddled together on the slope of a rocky spur 440 feet above

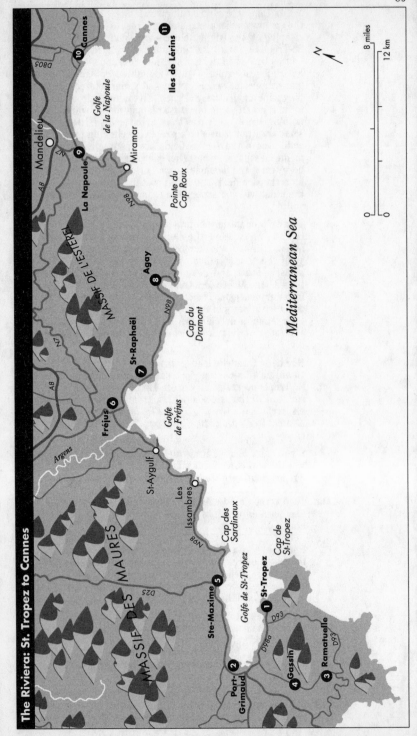

The Riviera: St. Tropez to Cannes

Cannes

Mandelieu

Iles de Lérins

Golfe de la Napoule

Miramar

Pointe du Cap Roux

La Napoule

Agay

MASSIF DE L'ESTÉREL

St-Raphaël

Cap du Dramont

Fréjus

Golfe de Fréjus

Argens

St-Aygulf

Les Issambres

Cap des Sardinaux

Golfe de St-Tropez

MASSIF DES MAURES

Ste-Maxime

Port-Grimaud

St-Tropez

Cap de St-Tropez

Gassin

Ramatuelle

Mediterranean Sea

8 miles

12 km

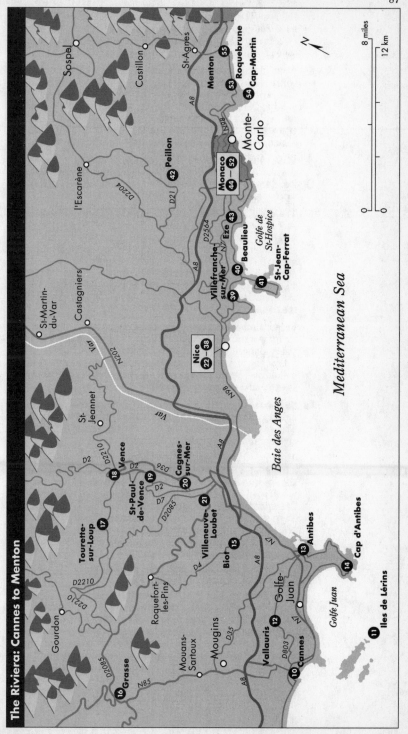

The Riviera: Cannes to Menton

Mediterranean Sea

Baie des Anges

Golfe Juan

Golfe de St-Hospice

Sospel

Castillon

St-Agnes

55 Roquebrune

53 Menton

54 Cap-Martin

l'Escarène

42 Peillon

Monte-Carlo

44 – 52 Monaco

43 Eze

40 Beaulieu

Villefranche-sur-Mer

39

41 St-Jean-Cap-Ferrat

St-Martin-du-Var

Castagniers

St-Jeannet

Var

22 – 38 Nice

Gourdon

Tourette-sur-Loup **17**

Vence **18**

St-Paul-de-Vence **19**

Cagnes-sur-Mer **20**

21 Villeneuve-Loubet

Roquefort-les-Pins

15 Biot

Grasse **16**

Mouans-Sartoux

Mougins

13 Antibes

14 Cap d'Antibes

11 Iles de Lérins

Golfe-Juan

12 Vallauris

10 Cannes

D2210

D2085

N85

D2210

D2

D2210

D2

D36

D2

D7

D2085

D4

D35

D803

N7

A8

A8

A8

N202

N202

A8

D21

D2204

D2204

D256d

N7

N98

N98

N7

D2

8 miles

12 km

N

the sea. The central square has a 17th-century church and a huge 300-year-old elm. Surrounding the square are narrow, twisting streets with medieval archways and vaulted passages.

❹ From Ramatuelle, follow signs to the old village of **Gassin,** which is less than 3 kilometers (2 miles) away. The ride through vineyards and woods is lovely, and takes you over the highest point of the peninsula (1,070 feet), where you can stop and enjoy a splendid view. The perched village of Gassin, with its venerable old houses and 12th-century Romanesque church, has somehow managed to maintain its medieval appearance.

D98a runs 6 kilometers (4 miles) west from St-Tropez, joining the major coastal highway, N98, which proceeds eastward 8 ki-
❺ lometers (5 miles) to **Ste-Maxime**—a family resort with a fine sandy beach.

The coastline between Ste-Maxime and Cannes consists of a succession of bays and beaches. Minor resorts have sprung up wherever nature permits—curious mixtures of lush villas,
❻ campsites, and fast-food stands. **Fréjus,** 19 kilometers (12 miles) farther along N98, was founded by Julius Caesar as Forum Julii in 49 BC, and it is thought that the Roman city grew to 40,000 people—10,000 more than the population today. The Roman remains are unspectacular, if varied, and consist of part of the theater, an arena, an aqueduct, and city walls.

Fréjus Cathedral dates from the 10th century, although the richly worked choir stalls belong to the 15th century. The baptistry alongside it, square on the outside and octagonal inside, is thought to date from AD 400, making it one of France's oldest buildings. The adjacent cloisters feature an unusual contrast between round and pointed arches.

❼ **St-Raphaël,** next door to Fréjus, is another family resort with holiday camps, best known to tourists as the railway stop to St-Tropez. It was here that the Allied forces landed in their offensive against the Germans in August 1944.

The rugged Massif de l'Estérel, between Fréjus and Cannes, is a hiker's joy, made up of volcanic rocks (porphyry) carved by the sea into dreamlike shapes. The harshness of the landscape is softened by patches of lavender, cane apple, and gorse. The deep gorges with sculpted, parasol pines could have inspired Tang and Sung Dynasty landscape painters. Drivers can take N7, the mountain route to the north or, as we propose, stay on the N98 coast road past tiny rust-colored beaches and sheer rock faces plunging into the sea.

Some 10 kilometers (6 miles) from St-Raphaël is the resort of
❽ **Agay,** whose deep bay was once used by traders from ancient Greece. Agay has the best-protected anchorage along the coast. It was here that writer Antoine de Saint-Exupéry *(The Little Prince)* was shot down in July 1944, having just flown
❾ over his family castle on his last mission. **La Napoule,** 24 kilometers (15 miles) from Agay, forms a unit with the older, inland village of **Mandelieu.** The village explodes with color during the Fête du Mimosa in February and boasts extensive modern sports facilities (swimming, boating, waterskiing, deep-sea diving, fishing, golf, tennis, horseback riding, and parachuting).

Art lovers will want to stop in La Napoule at the **Château de la Napoule Art Foundation** to see the eccentric work of the American sculptor Henry Clews. A cynic and sadist, Clews had, as one critic remarked, a knowledge of anatomy worthy of Michelangelo and the bizarre imagination of Edgar Allan Poe. *Av. Henry-Clews. Admission: 25 frs. Guided visits Mar.–Nov., Wed.–Mon., at 3, 4, and 5; Dec.–Feb., at 3 and 4.*

Cosmopolitan, sophisticated, smart—these are words that describe the most lively and flourishing city on the Riviera, 6 kilometers (4 miles) farther up the coast. **Cannes** is a resort town—unlike Nice, which is a city—that exists only for the pleasure of its guests. It's a tasteful and expensive breeding ground for the upscale (and those who are already "up"), a sybaritic heaven for those who believe that life is short and sin has something to do with the absence of a tan.

Alongside the long, narrow beach is a broad, elegant promenade called La Croisette, bordered by palm trees and flowers. At one end of the promenade is the modern Festival Hall, a summer casino, and an old harbor where pleasure boats are moored. At the other end is a winter casino and a modern harbor for some of the most luxurious yachts in the world. All along the promenade are cafés, boutiques, and luxury hotels like the Carlton and the Majestic. Speedboats and waterskiers glide by; little waves lick the beach, lined with prostrate bodies. Behind the promenade lies the town, filled with shops, restaurants, and hotels, and behind the town are the hills with the villas of the very rich.

The first thing to do is stroll along **La Croisette,** stopping at cafés and boutiques along the way. Near the eastern end (turning left as you face the water), before you reach the new port, is the **Parc de la Roserie,** where some 14,000 roses nod their heads in the wind. Walking west takes you past the **Palais des Festivals** (Festival Hall), where the famous film festival is held each May. Just past the hall is **Place du Général-de-Gaulle,** while on your left is the **old port.** If you continue straight beyond the port on Allées de la Liberté, you'll reach a tree-shaded area, where flowers are sold in the morning, boules is played in the afternoon, and a flea market is held on Saturday. If instead of continuing straight from the square you turn inland, you'll quickly come to rue Meynadier. Turn left. This is the old main street, which has many 18th-century houses—now boutiques and specialty food shops, where you can buy exotic foods and ship them.

You may want to visit the peaceful **Iles de Lérins** (Lerin Islands) to escape the crowds. The ferry leaves from Cannes Harbor (near the Palais des Festivals) and takes 15 minutes to **Ste-Marguerite,** 30 to **St-Honorat** (tel. 93–39–11–82 for information).

Ste-Marguerite, the larger of the two, is an island of wooded hills, with a tiny main street lined with fishermen's houses. Visitors enjoy peaceful walks through a forest of enormous eucalyptus trees and parasol pines. Paths wind through a dense undergrowth of tree heathers, rosemary, and thyme. The main attraction is the dank cell in **Fort Royal,** where the Man in the Iron Mask was imprisoned (1687–98) before going to the Bastille, where he died in 1703. The mask, which he always wore, was in fact made of velvet. Was he the illegitimate brother of Louis XIV or Louis XIII's son-in-law? No one knows.

St-Honorat is less tamed but more tranquil than its sister island. It was named for a hermit-monk who came here to escape his followers; but when the hermit founded a monastery here in AD 410, his disciples followed and the monastery became one of the most powerful in all Christendom. It's worth taking the two-hour walk around the island to the **old fortified monastery**, where noble Gothic arcades are arranged around a central courtyard. Next door to the "new" 19th-century monastery (open on request) is a shop where the monks sell handicrafts, lavender scent, and a home-brewed liqueur called Lerina. *Monastère de Lérins. Admission free. Open May–Oct., daily 9:45–4:30; Nov.–Apr. 10:45–3:30. High mass at the abbey 10:45 Sun.*

From Cannes, take D803 northeast to the pottery-making center of **Vallauris,** 5 kilometers (3 miles) away. Pottery is on sale throughout the village, and several workshops can be visited. Picasso spurred a resurgence of activity when he settled here in 1947 and created some whimsically beautiful ceramics. He also decorated the tunnel-like medieval chapel of the former priory with a fresco entitled *War and Peace. Pl. de la Mairie. Admission: 8 frs. Open Wed.–Mon. 10–noon and 2–6 (until 5 in winter); closed Tues.*

From Vallauris, continue east to **Antibes,** founded as a Greek trading port in the 4th century BC and now a center for fishing and rose growing. Avenue de l'Amiral-Grasse runs along the seafront from the harbor to the **marketplace,** a colorful sight most mornings, and to the church of the **Immaculate Conception,** with intricately carved portals (dating from 1710) and a 1515 altarpiece by Nice artist Louis Bréa (c. 1455–1523).

The **Château Grimaldi,** built in the 12th century by the ruling family of Monaco and extensively rebuilt in the 16th century, is reached by nearby steps. Tear yourself away from the sun-baked terrace overlooking the sea to go inside to the Picasso Museum. There are stone Roman remains on exhibit, but the works of Picasso—who occupied the château during his most cheerful and energetic period—hold center stage; they include an array of paintings, pottery, and lithographs inspired by the sea and Greek mythology. *Pl. du Château. Admission: 20 frs. adults, 10 frs. students and senior citizens. Open Dec.–Oct., Wed.–Mon. 10–noon and 2–6; closed Tues.*

Continue down avenue de l'Amiral-Grasse to the St-André Bastion, constructed by Sébastien de Vauban in the late 17th century and home to the **Musée Archéologique.** Here 4,000 years of local history are illustrated by continually expanding displays. *Bastion St-André. Admission: 10 frs. adults, 5 frs. children and senior citizens. Open Dec.–Oct., weekdays 9–noon and 2–6; closed weekends.*

Antibes officially forms one town (dubbed "Juantibes") with the more recent resort of **Juan-les-Pins** to the south, where beach and nightlife attract a younger and less affluent crowd than in Cannes. In the summer, the mood is especially frenetic.

The **Cap d'Antibes** peninsula is rich and residential, with beaches, views, and large villas hidden in luxurious vegetation. Barely two miles long by a mile wide, it offers a perfect day's outing. An ideal walk is along the **Sentier des Douaniers,** the customs officers' path.

From Pointe Bacon there is a striking view over the Baie des Anges (Bay of Angels) toward Nice; climb up to the nearby Plateau de la Garoupe for a sweeping view inland over the Esterel massif and the Alps. The **Sanctuaire de la Garoupe** (sailors' chapel) has a 14th-century icon, a statue of Our Lady of Safe Homecoming, and numerous frescoes and votive offerings. The lighthouse alongside, which can be visited, has a powerful beam that carries over 40 miles out to sea. *Admission free. Open Nov.–Mar., daily 10:30–12:30 and 2:30–7:30; Apr.–Oct., daily 10:30–12:30 and 2–5.*

Nearby is the **Jardin Thuret,** established by botanist Gustave Thuret (1817–75) in 1856 as France's first garden for subtropical plants and trees. The garden, now run by the Ministry of Agriculture, remains a haven for rare, exotic plants. *Blvd. du Cap. Admission free. Open weekdays 8–12:30 and 2–5:30.*

At the southwest tip of the peninsula, opposite the luxurious Grand Hôtel du Cap d'Antibes (*see* Dining and Lodging, below), is the **Musée Naval & Napoléonien,** a former battery, where you can spend an interesting hour scanning Napoleonic proclamations and viewing scale models of oceangoing ships. *Batterie du Grillon, blvd. du Maréchal-Juin. Admission: 15 frs. adults, 7 frs. children and senior citizens. Open Oct.–Apr., Wed.–Mon. 10–noon and 3–7; Dec.–Mar., Wed.–Mon. 9–noon and 2–6; closed Tues.*

Marineland, Europe's first aquatic zoo, is only a short distance from Antibes. Take N7 north and then head left at La Brague onto D4; Marineland is on the right. Performing dolphins leap into action every afternoon, abetted by a supporting cast of seals, penguins, and sea lions. There is also an amusement park. *309 rue Mozart. Admission: 84 frs. adults, 55 frs. children. Open Apr.–Oct., daily 10–9; Nov.–Mar., daily 11–6; first performance at 2:30.*

Mimosa and roses for the cut-flower market are grown at the charming old village of **Biot,** 4 kilometers (2½ miles) up D4. The glassworks at the edge of the village welcomes visitors to observe its glassblowers, but it is wise to call first to check opening times, which vary. *Verrerie de Biot, 5 chemin des Combes, tel. 93–65–03–00.*

Artist Fernand Léger (1881–1955) lived in Biot, and hundreds of his paintings, ceramics, and tapestries are on display at the museum here. Léger's stylistic evolution is traced from his early flirtation with Cubism to his ultimate preference for flat expanses of primary color and shades of gray, separated by thick black lines. *Chemin du Val de Pomme. Admission: 30 frs. adults, 15 frs. students and senior citizens, children free. Open Apr.–Oct., Tues.–Sun. 10–noon and 2–6; Nov.–Mar., 10–noon and 2–5.*

Tour 2: Grasse to Menton

Our tour of the eastern Riviera begins a dozen miles inland at **Grasse.** If you are coming from Cannes or Antibes, stop off en route to admire the dramatic hilltop setting of **Mougins,** a quaint, fortified town just north of Cannes.

If touring a perfume factory in a tacky modern town is your idea of pleasure, by all means visit Grasse. If you had visited four centuries ago, when the town specialized in leatherwork, you would have come for gloves. In the 16th century, when scented gloves became the rage, the town began cultivating flowers and distilling essences. That was the beginning of the perfume industry. Today some three-fourths of the world's essences are made here from wild lavender, jasmine, violets, daffodils, and other sweet-smelling flowers. Five thousand producers supply some 20 factories and six cooperatives. If you've ever wondered why perfume is so expensive, consider that it takes 10,000 flowers to produce 2.2 pounds of jasmine petals and that nearly one ton of jasmine is needed—nearly 7 million flowers—to distill 1½ quarts of essence. Sophisticated Parisian perfumers mix Grasse essences into their own secret formulas; perfumes made and sold in Grasse are considerably less subtle. You can, of course, buy Parisian perfumes in Grasse—at Parisian prices.

Several perfume houses welcome visitors for a whiff of their products and an explanation of how the perfumes are made: Galimard (73 rte. de Cannes, tel. 93–09–20–00); Molinard (60 blvd. Victor-Hugo, tel. 93–36–01–62); and Fragonard (20 blvd. Fragonard, tel. 93–36–44–65), which is conveniently central and has its own museum. All perfume houses invite you to purchase their products. *Admission to perfume houses free. Open daily 9–noon and 2–6.*

A new perfume museum, the **Musée International de la Parfumerie,** was opened in early 1989 and explains the history and manufacturing process of perfume. Old machinery, pots, and flasks can be admired; toiletry, cosmetics, and makeup accessories are on display; and there is a section devoted to perfume's sophisticated marketing aids, with examples of packaging and advertising posters. *8 pl. du Cours. Admission: 12 frs. adults, 6 frs. children and senior citizens. Open Wed.–Mon. 10–6; closed Tues.*

The artist Jean-Honoré Fragonard (1732–1806) was born in Grasse, and many of his pictures, etchings, drawings, and sketches—plus others by his son Alexandre-Evariste and his grandson Théophile—are hung in the 17th-century Villa Fragonard, situated close to the perfumerie of the same name. *23 blvd. Fragonard, tel. 93–36–01–61. Admission: 8 frs. adults, 4 frs. children and senior citizens. Joint ticket for all Grasse museums: 22 frs. adults, 11 frs. children and senior citizens. Open Wed.–Sun. 10–noon and 2–5; closed Mon. and Tues.*

The **Musée d'Art et d'Histoire de Provence,** around the corner on rue Mirabeau, is in an 18th-century mansion. It houses a collection of Provençal furniture, folk art, tools and implements, and china. *2 rue Mirabeau. Admission: 8 frs. adults, 4 frs. children and senior citizens. Open Apr.–Oct., Mon.–Sat. 10–noon and 2–6; Dec.–Mar., 10–noon and 2–5.*

From Grasse, strike east along D2085/D2210 toward Vence, 25 kilometers (16 miles) away. About 5 kilometers (3 miles) before you reach Vence is **Tourette-sur-Loup**, whose outer houses form a rampart on a rocky plateau, 1,300 feet above a valley full of violets. The town is much less commercialized than many others in the area; its shops are filled not with postcards and scented soaps but with the work of dedicated artisans. A rough stone path takes you on a circular route around the rim of the town, past the shops of engravers, weavers, potters, and painters. Ask any artisan for a map of the town that locates each of the shops. Also worth visiting is a single-nave 14th-century church that has a notable wooden altarpiece.

18 When you arrive in **Vence,** leave your car on avenue Foch and climb up to the medieval town (Vieille Ville). The Romans were the first to settle on the 1,000-foot hill; the **cathedral** (built between the 11th and 18th centuries), rising above the medieval ramparts and traffic-free streets, was erected on the site of a temple to Mars. Of special note are a mosaic by Marc Chagall of Moses in the bullrushes and the ornate 15th-century wooden choir stalls.

At the foot of the hill, on the outskirts of Vence, is the **Chapelle du Rosaire,** a small chapel decorated with beguiling simplicity and clarity by Matisse between 1947 and 1951. The walls, floor, and ceiling are gleaming white and are pierced by small stained-glass windows in cool greens and blues. "Despite its imperfections I think it is my masterpiece . . . the result of a lifetime devoted to the search for truth," wrote Matisse, who designed and dedicated the chapel when he was in his eighties and nearly blind. *Av. Henri-Matisse. Admission free. Open Tues. and Thur. 10–11:30 and 2:30–5:30.*

19 A few miles south along D2 is **St-Paul-de-Vence,** a gem of a town whose medieval atmosphere has been perfectly preserved. Not even the hordes of tourists—to which the village now caters—can destroy its ancient charm. You can walk the narrow, cobbled streets in perhaps 15 minutes, but you'll need another hour to explore the shops—mostly galleries selling second-rate landscape paintings, but also a few serious studios and gift shops offering everything from candles to dolls, dresses, and hand-dipped chocolate strawberries. Your best bet is to visit in the late afternoon, when the tour buses are gone, and enjoy a drink among the Klees and Picassos in the Colombe d'Or (*see* Dining and Lodging, *below*). Be sure to visit the remarkable 12th-century Gothic church; you'll want to light a candle to relieve its wonderful gloom. The treasury is rich in 12th–15th-century pieces, including processional crosses, reliquaries, and an enamel Virgin and Child.

At La Gardette, just northwest of the village, is the **Fondation Maeght,** one of the world's most famous small museums of modern art. Monumental sculptures are scattered around its pine-tree park, and a courtyard full of Alberto Giacometti's elongated creations separates the two museum buildings. The rooms inside showcase the works of Joan Miró, Georges Braque, Wassily Kandinsky, Bonnard, Matisse and others. Few museums blend form and content so tastefully and imaginatively. There is also a library, movie theater, and auditorium. *Admission: 35 frs. adults, 25 frs. children. Open Apr.–Oct., daily 10–7; Nov.–Mar., daily 10–12:30 and 2:30–6.*

20 Return to D2 and continue 6 kilometers (4 miles) south to **Cagnes-sur-Mer.** An attractive **château,** once a medieval fortress, is perched high above the modern seaside resort within the walls of Haut-de-Cagnes, the old town. Much of the château's Renaissance decoration—frescoes, plasterwork, and fireplaces—remains intact, and the third floor hosts an art gallery devoted to Mediterranean artists, including Chagall and Raoul Dufy. There's an exciting panorama from the top of the tower. *Pl. du Château. Admission: 6 frs. adults, 3 frs. stu-*

dents. *Open Easter–mid-Oct., daily 10–noon and 2:30–7; mid-Nov.–Easter, Wed.–Mon. 10–noon and 2–5, closed Tues.*

The painter Auguste Renoir (1841–1919) spent the last years of his life at Cagnes. His home at Les Collettes has been preserved, and you can see his studio, as well as some of his work. A bronze statue of Venus nestles amid the fruit trees in the colorful garden. *Av. des Collettes. Admission: 20 frs. adults, 10 frs. children. Open Apr.–Oct., daily 2:30–6:30; Nov.–Mar., Wed.–Mon. 2–5.*

㉑ A mile west of Cagnes is the tiny village of **Villeneuve-Loubet,** worth visiting for its **Fondation Escoffier:** a gourmet shrine that can be fitted in between meals because there's nothing to eat. As kitchen overlord at the London Carlton and the Paris Ritz, Auguste Escoffier (1846–1935) carved out a reputation as Europe's top chef. One of his inventions is Peach Melba. This museum, in the house where he was born, displays some elaborate *pièces montées* in sugar and marzipan and boasts a lip-smacking collection of 15,000 menus. *3 rue Escoffier. Admission: 14 frs. adults, 7 frs. students. Open Dec.–Oct., Tues.–Sun. 2–6.*

The congested N7 from Cagnes to Nice is enough to put you off the Riviera for life. Tedious concrete constructions assault the eye; the railroad, on one side, and the stony shore, on the other, offer scant respite. Soon, however, you'll arrive at the Queen of **㉒** the Riviera—**Nice.**

Nice is less glamorous, less sophisticated, and less expensive than Cannes. It's also older—weathered-old and faded-old—like a wealthy dowager who has seen better days but still maintains a demeanor of dignity and poise. Nice is a big, sprawling city of 350,000 people—five times as many as Cannes—and has a life and vitality that survive when tourists pack their bags and go home.

Nice is worth a visit, but should you stay here? On the negative side, its beaches are cramped and pebbly. Many of its hotels are either rundown or being refurbished for the convention crowd. On the positive side, Nice is likely to have hotel space, at prices you can afford, when all other towns are full. It's also a convenient base from which to explore Monte Carlo and the medieval towns in the interior. It does have its share of first-class restaurants and boutiques, and an evening stroll through the old town or along the Promenade des Anglais is something to savor.

Numbers in the margin correspond to points of interest on the Nice map.

We suggest that you divide your visit of Nice into three **㉓** minitours, with arcaded **place Masséna,** the city's main square, as a common starting point. First, head west through the foun- **㉔ ㉕** tains and gardens of the **Jardin Albert I** to the **Promenade des Anglais,** built, as the name indicates, by the English community in 1824. Traffic on this multilane highway can be heavy, but once you have crossed to the seafront, there are fine views, across private beaches, of the Baie des Anges.

Time Out Walk as far as the Neptune Plage (beach) and cross over to the **Hôtel Negresco.** If you can't afford to stay here, spend a few dollars on a cup of coffee and think of it as an admission charge to this palatial hotel. *37 promenade des Anglais.*

95

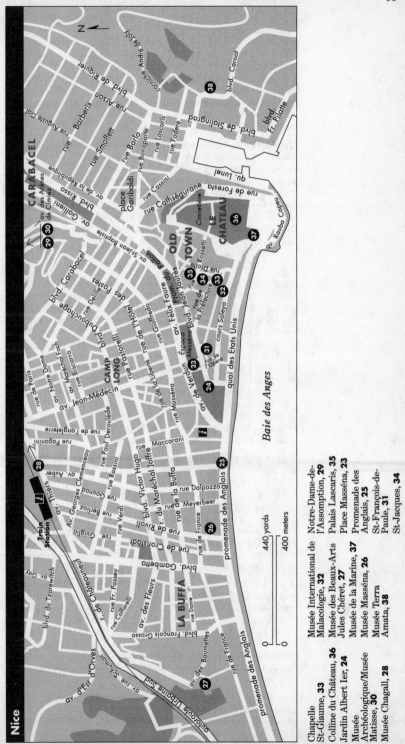

Nice

CARABACEL

OLD TOWN

LE CHATEAU

CAMP LONG

LA BUFFA

Train Station

Baie des Anges

0 — 440 yards
0 — 400 meters

Chapelle
St-Giaume, **33**
Colline du Château, **36**
Jardin Albert Ier, **24**
Musée
Archéologique/Musée
Matisse, **30**
Musée Chagall, **28**

Musée International de
Malacologie, **32**
Musée des Beaux-Arts
Jules Chéret, **27**
Musée de la Marine, **37**
Musée Masséna, **26**
Musée Terra
Amata, **38**

Notre-Dame-de-
l'Assomption, **29**
Palais Lascaris, **35**
Place Masséna, **23**
Promenade des
Anglais, **25**
St-François-de-
Paule, **31**
St-Jacques, **34**

㉖ Just up rue de Rivoli from the Hôtel Negresco is the **Musée Masséna,** concerned principally with the Napoleonic era and, in particular, with the life of local-born general André Masséna (1756–1817). Bonaparte rewarded the general for his heroic exploits during the Italian campaign with the sonorous sobriquet *l'Enfant chéri de la victoire* (the Cherished Child of Victory). Sections of the museum evoke the history of Nice and its carnival; there are also some fine Renaissance paintings and objects. *67 rue de France. Admission free. Open Tues.–Sun. 10–noon and 2–5; closed 2 weeks in Nov. or Dec.*

Head left along rue de France, then turn right up avenue des
㉗ Baumettes to the **Musée des Beauxe Arts Jules Chéret,** Nice's fine-arts museum, built in 1878 as a palatial mansion for a Russian princess. The rich collection of paintings includes works by Auguste Renoir, Edgar Degas, Claude Monet, and Raoul Dufy; Oriental prints; sculptures by Auguste Rodin; and ceramics by Picasso. Jules Chéret (1836–1932) is best known for his Belle Epoque posters; several of his oils, pastels, and tapestries can be admired here. *33 av. des Baumettes. Admission free. Open May–Sept., Tues.–Sun. 10–noon and 3–6; Oct. and Dec.–Apr., Tues.–Sun. 10–noon and 2–5.*

Nice's main shopping street, avenue Jean-Médecin, runs inland from place Masséna; all needs and most tastes are catered to in its big department stores (Nouvelles Galeries, Prisunic, and the split-level Etoile mall). Continue past the train station, on
㉘ avenue Thiers, then take the first right down to the **Musée Chagall**—built to show off the paintings of Marc Chagall (1887–1985) in natural light. The Old Testament is the primary subject of the works, which include 17 huge canvases covering a period of 13 years, together with 195 preliminary sketches, several sculptures, and nearly 40 gouaches. In summertime, you can buy snacks and drinks in the garden. *Av. du Dr-Ménard. Admission: 17 frs. adults, 9 frs. children and senior citizens and on Sun. Open July–Sept., Wed.–Mon. 10–7; Oct.–July, Wed.–Mon. 10–12:30 and 2–5.30.*

Boulevard de Cimiez heads to the residential quarter of Nice—the hilltop site of **Cimiez,** occupied by the Romans 2,000 years ago. The foundations of the Roman town can be seen, along with vestiges of the arena, less spectacular than those at Arles or Nîmes but still in use (notably for a summer jazz festival).
㉙ Close by is the Franciscan monastery of **Notre-Dame-de-l'Assomption,** with some outstanding late-medieval religious pictures; guided tours include the small museum and an audiovisual show on the life and work of the Franciscans. *Admission free. Open weekdays 10–noon and 3–6.*

A 17th-century Italian villa amid the Roman remains contains
㉚ two museums: the **Musée Archéologique,** with a plethora of ancient objects, and the **Musée Matisse,** with paintings and bronzes by Henri Matisse (1869–1954), illustrating the different stages of his career. The Matisse Museum is scheduled to reopen in 1993 after a five-year renovation program. *164 av. des Arènes-de-Cimiez, tel. 93–53–17–70. Admission free. Open May–Sept., 10–noon and 2:30–6:30; Oct.–Apr., 10–noon and 2–5.*

The **old town** of Nice is one of the delights of the Riviera. Cars are forbidden on streets that are so narrow that their buildings crowd out the sky. The winding alleyways are lined with faded

17th- and 18th-century buildings, where families sell their wares. Flowers cascade from window boxes on soft pastel-colored walls. You wander down cobbled streets, proceeding with the logic of dreams, or sit in an outdoor café on a Venetian-looking square, basking in the purest, most transparent light.

To explore the old town, head south from place Masséna along rue de l'Opéra, and turn left into rue St-François-de-Paule. **㉛** You'll soon come to the 18th-century church of **St-François-de-Paule,** renowned for its ornate Baroque interior and sculpted decoration.

Time Out   Shop for the best crystallized fruits in Nice at **Henri Auer** (7 rue St-François-de-Paule) and have an ice cream and pastry in his cozy tearoom.

Rue St-François-de-Paule becomes the pedestrian-only cours Saleya, with its colorful morning market selling seafood, flowers, and orange trees in tubs. Toward the far end of cours **㉜** Saleya is the **Musée International de Malacologie,** with a collection of seashells from all over the world (some for sale) and a small aquarium of Mediterranean sea life. *3 cours Saleya. Admission free. Open Dec.–Oct., Tues.–Sat. 10:30–1 and 2–6.*

㉝ Next, stroll left up rue la Poissonnerie and pop into the **Chapelle St-Giaume** to admire its gleaming Baroque interior and grand altarpieces. Continue to rue de Jésus; at one end is the **㉞** church of **St-Jacques,** featuring an explosion of painted angels **㉟** on the ceiling. Walk along rue Droite to the elegant **Palais Lascaris,** built in the mid-17th century and decorated with paintings and tapestries. The palace boasts a particularly grand staircase and a reconstructed 18th-century pharmacy. *15 rue Droite. Admission free. Open Dec.–Oct., Tues.–Sun. 9:30–noon and 2–6.*

㊱ Old Nice is dominated by the **Colline du Château** (Castle Hill), a romantic cliff fortified many centuries before Christ. The ruins of a 6th-century castle can be explored and the views from the **㊲** surrounding garden admired. A small naval museum, the **Musée de la Marine,** is situated in the 16th-century tower known as the **Tour Bellanda,** with models, instruments, and documents charting the history of the port of Nice. *Rue du Château, tel. 93–80–47–61. Admission free. Open Apr.–Sept., Wed.–Mon. 10–noon and 2–7; Oct.–Mar., Wed.–Mon. 10–noon and 2–5; closed Tues.*

The elevator between Tour Bellanda and the quayside operates daily 9 until 7 in summer and 2 until 7 in winter. The back of Castle Hill overlooks the harbor. On the other side, along bou- **㊳** levard Carnot, is the **Musée Terra Amata,** containing relics of a local settlement that was active 400,000 years ago. There are recorded commentaries in English and films explaining the lifestyle of prehistoric dwellers. *25 blvd. Carnot, tel. 93–55– 59– 93. Admission free. Open Tues.–Sun. 9–noon and 2–6; closed second half of Sept.*

There are three scenic roads at various heights above the coast between Nice and Monte Carlo, a distance of about 19 kilometers (12 miles). All are called "corniches"—literally, a projecting molding along the top of a building or wall. The **Basse** (lower) **Corniche** is the busiest and slowest route because it passes through all the coastal towns. The **Moyenne** (middle)

Corniche is high enough for views and close enough for details. It passes the perched village of Eze. The **Grande** (upper) **Corniche** winds some 1,300 to 1,600 feet above the sea, offering sweeping views of the coast. The Grande Corniche follows the Via Aurelia, the great Roman military road that brought Roman legions from Italy to Gaul (France). In 1806, Napoleon rebuilt the road and sent Gallic troops into Italy. The best advice is to take the Moyenne Corniche one way and the Grande Corniche the other. The view from the upper route is best in the early morning or evening.

Numbers in the margin correspond to points of interest on the Riviera maps.

㊴ Boulevard Carnot becomes the popular, pretty Basse Corniche (N98), which crawls along the coast from Nice to **Villefranche-sur-Mer,** 4 kilometers (2½ miles) east. The harbor town is a miniature version of old Marseille, with steep narrow streets—one, **rue Obscure,** an actual tunnel—winding down to the sea. The town is a stage set of brightly colored houses—orange buildings with lime-green shutters, yellow buildings with ice-blue shutters—the sort of place where *Fanny* could have been filmed. If you're staying in Nice, include Villefranche on a tour of Cap Ferrat. To see the Cocteau Chapel you'll need to arrive by 4 PM. If you skip the chapel, your best bet is to come at sundown (for dinner, perhaps) and enjoy an hour's walk around the harbor, when the sun turns the soft pastels to gold.

The 17th-century **St-Michel** church has a strikingly realistic Christ, carved of boxwood by an unknown convict. The chapel of St-Pierre-des-Pêcheurs, known as the **Cocteau Chapel,** is a small Romanesque chapel once used for storing fishing nets, which the French writer and painter Jean Cocteau decorated in 1957. Visitors walk through the flames of the Apocalypse (represented by staring eyes on either side of the door) and enter a room filled with frescoes of St. Peter, Gypsies, and the women of Villefranche. *Admission: 10 frs. Open May–Oct., daily 9–noon and 2–4:30; Nov.–Apr., daily 9–noon and 2:30–7.*

㊵ **Beaulieu** is just next door to Villefranche, a place for high society at the turn of the century. Stop and walk along the promenade, sometimes called Petite Afrique (Little Africa) because of its magnificent palm trees, to get a flavor of how things used to be.

The one thing to do in Beaulieu is visit the **Villa Kérylos.** In the early part of the century, a rich amateur archaeologist named Theodore Reinach asked an Italian architect to build an authentic Greek house for him. The villa, now open to the public, is a faithful reproduction, made from cool Carrara marble, alabaster, and rare fruitwoods. The furniture, made of wood inlaid with ivory, bronze, and leather, was copied from drawings of Greek interiors found on ancient vases and mosaics. *Admission: 20 frs. adults, 10 frs. children and senior citizens. Open July–Aug., daily 3–7; Sept.–June, Tues.–Sun. 2–6.*

㊶ From Beaulieu, make a detour along D25 around the lush peninsula of **St-Jean-Cap-Ferrat** and visit the 17-acre gardens and richly varied art collection of the **Musée Ephrussi de Rothschild.** The museum reflects the sensibilities of its former owner, Madame Ephrussi de Rothschild, sister of Baron Edouard de Rothschild. An insatiable collector, she surrounded herself with an eclectic but tasteful collection of Impressionist paintings, Louis XIII furniture, rare Sèvres porcelain, and objets d'art from the Far East. *Villa Ile-de-France, tel. 93–01–33–09. Admission: 28 frs. adults, 17 frs. students, children free. Guided tours only. Open Dec.–Oct., Tues.–Sat. 10–noon and 2–6, Sun. and winter 2–6; closed Nov.*

42 The perched village of **Peillon** is about 10 kilometers (6 miles) inland from Nice. Take D2204, turn right on D21, and turn right again, up the mountain. Of all the perched villages along the Riviera, Peillon a fortified medieval town situated on a craggy mountaintop more than 1,000 feet above the sea, is the most spectacular and the least spoiled. Unchanged since the Middle Ages, the village has only a few narrow streets and many steps and covered alleys. There's really nothing to do here but look—which is why the tour buses stay away, leaving Peillon uncommercialized for the 50 families who live there—including professionals summering away from Paris and artists who want to escape the craziness of the world below. Visit the **Chapel of the White Penitents** (key available at the Auberge); spend a half hour exploring the ancient streets, then head back down the mountain to Nice.

Time Out Have lunch or dinner at the charming **Auberge de la Madone,** a short walk from the chapel.

43 Almost every tour from Nice to Monaco includes a visit to the medieval hill town of **Eze,** perched on a rocky spur near the Middle Corniche, some 1,300 feet above the sea. (Don't confuse Eze with the beach town of **Eze-sur-Mer,** which is down by the water.) Be warned that because of its accessibility the town is also crowded and commercial: Eze has its share of serious craftspeople, but most of its vendors make their living selling perfumed soaps and postcards to the package-tour trade.

Enter through a fortified 14th-century gate and wander down narrow, cobbled streets with vaulted passageways and stairs. The church is 18th century, but the small Chapel of the White Penitents dates from 1306 and contains a 13th-century gilded wooden Spanish Christ and some notable 16th-century paintings. Tourist and crafts shops line the streets leading to the ruins of a castle, which has a scenic belvedere. Some of the most tasteful crafts shops are in the hotel/restaurant **Chèvre d'Or.**

Near the top of the village is a garden with exotic flowers and cacti. It's worth the admission price, but if you have time for only one exotic garden, visit the one in Monte Carlo.

If you're not going to Grasse, the perfume capital of the world (*see* above), consider visiting a branch of a Grasse perfumerie called **La Parfumerie Fragonard,** located in front of the public gardens.

44 From Eze it's just a short—albeit spectacular—drive up the coast to **Monaco.** The Principality of Monaco covers just 473 acres and would fit comfortably inside New York's Central Park or a family farm in Iowa. Its 5,000 citizens would fill only a small fraction of the seats in Yankee Stadium. The country is so tiny that residents have to go to another country to play golf.

The present ruler, Rainier III, traces his ancestry to Otto Canella, who was born in 1070. The Grimaldi dynasty began with Otto's great-great-great-grandson, Francesco Grimaldi, also known as Frank the Rogue. Expelled from Genoa, Frank and

his cronies disguised themselves as monks and seized the fortified medieval town known today as the Rock in 1297. Except for
a short break under Napoleon, the Grimaldis have been here
ever since, which makes them the oldest reigning family in Europe. On the Grimaldi coat of arms are two monks holding
swords (look up and you'll see them above the main door as you
enter the palace).

Back in the 1850s, a Grimaldi named Charles III made a deci-
sion that turned the Rock into a giant blue chip. Needing reve-
nues but not wanting to impose additional taxes on his subjects,
he contracted with a company to open a gambling facility. The
first spin of the roulette wheel was on December 14, 1856.
There was no easy way to reach Monaco then—no carriage
roads or railroads—so no one came. Between March 15 and
March 20, 1857, one person entered the casino—and won two
francs. In 1868, however, the railroad reached Monaco, filled
with wheezing Englishmen who came to escape the London
fog. The effects were immediate. Profits were so great that
Charles eventually abolished all direct taxes.

Almost overnight, a threadbare principality became an elegant
watering hole for European society. Dukes (and their mis-
tresses) and duchesses (and their gigolos) danced and dined
their way through a world of spinning roulette wheels and bub-
bling champagne—preening themselves for nights at the opera, where such artists as Vaslav Nijinsky, Sarah Bernhardt,
and Enrico Caruso came to perform.

Monte Carlo—the modern gambling town with elegant shops,
man-made beaches, high-rise hotels, and a few Belle Epoque
hotels—is actually only one of four parts of Monaco. The second is the medieval town on the Rock ("Old Monaco"), 200 feet
above the sea. It's here that Prince Rainier lives.

The third area is **La Condamine,** the commercial harbor area
with apartments and businesses. The fourth is **Fontvieille,** the
industrial district situated on 20 acres of reclaimed land.

*Numbers in the margin correspond to points of interest on the
Monaco map.*

Start at the Monte Carlo tourist office just north of the casino
gardens (ask for the useful English booklet *Getting Around in
the Principality).* The **Casino** is a must-see, even if you don't
bet a cent. You may find it fun to count the Jaguars and Rolls-
Royces parked outside and breathe on the windows of shops
selling Saint-Laurent dresses and fabulous jewels. Within the
gold-leaf splendor of the casino, where fortunes have been won
and shirts have been lost, the hopeful traipse in from tour buses
to tempt fate at the slot machines beneath the gilt-edged rococo
ceiling.

The main gambling hall, once called the European Room, has
been renamed the American Room and fitted with 150 one-
armed bandits from Chicago. Adjoining it is the Pink Salon,
now a bar where unclad nymphs float about on the ceiling smoking cigarillos. The Salles Privées (private rooms) are for high
rollers. The stakes are higher here, so the mood is more sober,
and well-wishers are herded farther back from the tables.

On July 17, 1924, black came up 17 times in a row on Table 5.
This was the longest run ever. A dollar left on black would have
grown to $131,072. On August 7, 1913, the number 36 came up

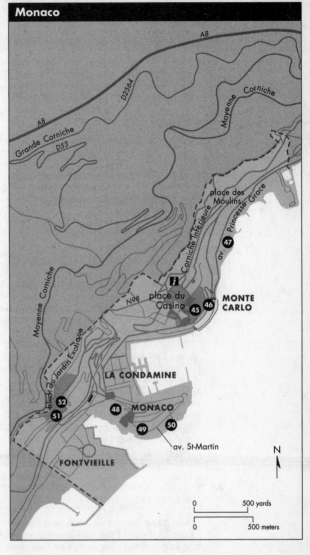

Monaco

three times in a row. In those days, if a gambler went broke, the casino bought him a ticket home.

The casino opens at 10 AM and continues until the last die is thrown. Ties and jackets are required in the back rooms, which open at 4 PM. Bring your passport.

Place du Casino is the center of Monte Carlo, and, in the true spirit of this place, it seems that the **Opera House,** with its 18-ton gilt bronze chandelier, is part of the casino complex. The designer, Charles Garnier, also built the Paris Opera.

46 The serious gamblers, some say, play at **Loew's Casino,** nearby. It opens weekdays at 4 PM and weekends at 1 PM. You may want to try parking here, since parking near the old casino is next to impossible in season.

From place des Moulins there is an escalator down to the Larvotto beach complex, artfully created with imported sand, and the **47** **Musée National,** housed in a Garnier villa within a rose garden. This museum has a beguiling collection of 18th- and 19th-century dolls and mechanical automatons, most in working order. *17 av. Princesse-Grace, tel. 93–30–91–26. Admission: 24 frs. adults, 14 frs. children. Open 10–12:15 and 2:30–6:30; closed holidays.*

Prince Rainier spends much of the year in his grand Italianate **48** **Palace** on the Rock. The changing of the guard takes place here each morning at 11:55, and the State Apartments can be visited in summer. *Admission: 25 frs. adults, 13 frs. children. Joint ticket with Musée Napoléon: 36 frs. adults, 18 frs. children. Open June–Oct., daily 9:30–6:30.*

One wing of the palace, open throughout the year, is taken up by a museum filled with Napoleonic souvenirs and documents related to Monaco's history. *Admission: 18 frs. adults, 9 frs. children. Joint ticket with palace apartments: 36 frs. adults, 18 frs. children. Open Tues.–Sun. 9:30–6:30.*

From here, a stroll through the medieval alleyways takes you **49** past the **cathedral,** a neo-Romanesque monstrosity (1875–84), with several important paintings of the Nice school. Continue **50** to one of Monaco's most outstanding showpieces, the **Musée Océanographique**—also an important research institute headed by celebrated underwater explorer and filmmaker Jacques Cousteau. Prince Rainier's great-grandfather Albert I (1848–1922), an accomplished marine biologist, founded the institute, which now boasts two exploration ships, laboratories, and a staff of 60 scientists. Nonscientific visitors may wish to make straight for the well-arranged and generously stocked aquarium in the basement. Other floors are devoted to Prince Albert's collection of seashells and whale skeletons and to Cousteau's diving equipment. *Av. St-Martin, tel. 93–15–36–00. Admission: 50 frs. adults, 25 frs. children. Open July–Aug., daily 9–9; Sept.–June, daily 9:30–7.*

Time Out Take the museum's elevator to the roof terrace for a fine view and a restorative drink.

A brisk half-hour walk back past the palace takes you to the **51** **Jardin Exotique** (Tropical Gardens), where 600 varieties of cac- **52** ti and succulents cling to a sheer rock face. The **Museum of Prehistoric Anthropology,** on the grounds, contains bones, tools, and other artifacts. Shapes of the stalactites and stalagmites in the cavernous grotto resemble the cacti outside. *Blvd. du Jardin Exotique. Admission: 32 frs. adults, 24 frs. senior citizens, 16 frs. children. Open daily 9–7 (dusk in winter).*

Numbers in the margin correspond to points of interest on the Riviera maps.

Five kilometers (3 miles) northeast of Monaco is the engaging **53** hilltop village of **Roquebrune,** with its steps and narrow **54** streets. The adjacent **Cap-Martin** peninsula is colonized by wealthy villa dwellers. Near the tip, on avenue Winston-Churchill, is the start of a coastal path—promenade Le Corbusier—that leads hardy ramblers to Monte Carlo in 1½ hours.

55 Next door to Roquebrune is **Menton,** a comparatively quiet all-year resort with the warmest climate on the Riviera. Lemon trees flourish here, as do senior citizens, enticed by a long strand of beaches. Menton likes to call itself the Pearl of the Riviera—beautiful, respectable, and not grossly expensive.

Walk eastward from the casino along promenade du Soleil to the harbor. There is a small 17th-century fort here, where writer, artist, and filmmaker Jean Cocteau (1889–1963) once worked. The fort now houses the **Cocteau Museum** of fantastic paintings, drawings, stage sets, and a large mosaic. *Bastion du Port, 111 quai Napoléon III. Admission free. Open Apr.–Oct., Wed–Sun. 10–noon and 2–6; Nov.–Mar., Wed.–Sun. 10–noon and 3–6; closed Mon. and Tues.*

The quaint old town above the jetty has an Italian feel to it. Visit the church of **St-Michel** for its ornate Baroque interior and altarpiece of St. Michael slaying a dragon. Concerts of chamber music are held in the square on summer nights.

Higher still is the **Vieux Cimetière** (old cemetery), with a magnificent view of the old town and coast. Here lie Victorian foreigners—Russians, Germans, English—who hoped (in vain, as the dates on the tombstones reveal) that Menton's balmy climate would reverse the ravages of tuberculosis.

Return to the center and the pedestrian rue St-Michel. On avenue de la République, which runs parallel, is the **Hôtel de Ville** (Town Hall). The room in which civil marriage ceremonies are conducted has vibrant allegorical frescoes by Cocteau; a tape in English helps to interpret them. *17 rue de la République. Admission free. Open weekdays 8:30–noon and 1:30– 5:45.*

Two other places of interest lie at opposite ends of Menton. To the west is the **Palais Carnolès,** an 18th-century villa once used as a summer retreat by the princes of Monaco. The gardens are beautiful, and the collection of European paintings (13th- to 18th-century) is extensive. *3 av. de la Madone. Admission free. Open Wed.–Sun. 10–noon and 2–6; closed holidays.*

At the other end of Menton, above the Garavan harbor, lie the **Colombières Gardens,** where follies and statues lurk among 15 acres of hedges, yew trees, and Mediterranean flowers. *Chemin de Valleya. Admission: 16 frs. Open Feb.–Sept., daily 9–noon and 3–8 (or sunset if earlier).*

The Italian frontier is just a mile away, and the first Italian town, **Ventimiglia** (Vintimille in French), is 10 kilometers (6 miles) beyond.

What to See and Do with Children

The **Jungle des Papillons,** opposite Marineland in Antibes, hosts a fluttering "Butterfly Ballet" that must be seen to be believed. Visitors are requested to wear colored clothing because this apparently stimulates the butterflies into a wing-flapping frenzy. *309 av. de Mozart, tel. 93–33–55–77. Admission 45 frs. adults, 35 frs. children. Open daily 10–5.*

The following attractions are described in Exploring the Riviera (*see above*):

Automatons at the Musée Nationale, Monte-Carlo, Tour 2
Glassblowers at Biot, Tour 1

Marineland, near Antibes, Tour 1

Musée Océanographique (Museum of Oceanography), Monte Carlo, Tour 2

Off the Beaten Track

Consider a visit to the Italian towns of Ventimiglia and San Remo by train, bus, or car; bring your passport. **Ventimiglia** lies just 10 kilometers (6 miles) over the border and is best known for its colorful Friday flower market, which draws huge crowds (mostly French). If you decide to visit on market day, take the train or bus; there will be no place to park. The elegant town of **San Remo,** just 6 kilometers (4 miles) farther down the coast, still maintains some of the glamour of its late-19th-century heyday; compare its casino with that of Monte Carlo. From October to June, you can visit Italy's most important flower market, the Mercato dei Fiori. The old town is an atmospheric warren of alleyways leading up to the piazza Castello, which features a splendid view of the old town.

Costumes, furniture, buildings, and even entire towns often evoke the stuff of heroes. Occasionally, so do roads—and one of the most famous roads in France is the **Route Napoléon,** taken by Napoleon Bonaparte in 1815 after his escape from imprisonment on the Mediterranean island of Elba. Napoleon landed at Golfe-Juan, near Cannes, on March 1 and forged northwest to Grasse and through dramatic, hilly countryside to Castellane, Digne, and Sisteron. In Napoleon's day, most of this "road" was little more than a winding dirt track, but now N85 allows drivers to mix history with scenery. Commemorative plaques bearing the imperial eagle stud the route, inspired by Napoleon's remark that "The eagle will fly from steeple to steeple until it reaches the towers of Notre-Dame." That prediction came true. Napoleon covered the 110 miles from the coast to Sisteron in just four days, romped north through Grenoble and Burgundy, and entered Paris in triumph on May 20.

One of the most spectacular roads in France is the **Corniche Sublime** (D71), which runs along the south side of the **Gorges du Verdon** (Verdon River Gorge), France's answer to the Grand Canyon. To reach the gorge, take the Route Napoléon (N85) from Grasse; turn left after 43 kilometers (27 miles) along D21, which becomes D71 at Comps-sur-Artuby. This is not a road for anyone who is afraid of heights. The narrow lane—just wide enough for two cars to scrape by—snakes its way for 25 miles along the cliffside, 3,000 feet above the tiny River Verdon. At times the river disappears from view beneath the sheer rock face. At the far end of the gorge you'll arrive at the sparkling blue Lac de Sainte-Croix.

Shopping

Clothes Cannes is one of the Riviera's top spots for chic clothing. Some of the most exclusive shops are **Chanel** (5 La Croisette), **Alexandra Scherra** (Rond-Point Duboys-d'Angers), **Cacharel** (16 rue des Belges), **Révillon** (45 La Croisette), and **St-Laurent** (44 La Croisette). For well-cut menswear, try **Cerruti** (15 rue des Serbes), **Christian Dior,** and **Francesco Smalto** (both at the Hôtel Gray Albion, 38 rue des Serbes).

Food Items Crystallized fruit is a Nice specialty; there's a terrific selection at **Henri Auer** (7 rue St-François-de-Paule). Locals and visitors alike buy olive oil by the gallon from tiny **Alziari**, just down the street at No. 14; the cans sport colorful, old-fashioned labels, and you can also pick up lots of Provençal herbs and spices. For cheese, try **l'Etable** (1 rue Sade) in Antibes. **Georget** (11 rue Allard), in St-Tropez, sells delicious handmade chocolates.

Markets St-Tropez's **place des Lices** has a clothing and antiques market on Tuesday and Saturday mornings. In addition to plants, Nice's famous flower market at **cours Saleya** also features mounds of fish, shellfish, and a host of other food items; on Monday, there's a flea market at the same spot. In Cannes, a market selling everything from strings of garlic to secondhand gravy boats is held on Saturday on **Allées de la Liberté.**

Sports and Fitness

La Napoule is the best place for the sports oriented. As well as facilities for boating, golf, horseback riding, and tennis, there are eight beaches with facilities for waterskiing and jet-skiing (there's a school on the plage du Sweet) and a deep-sea diving club (Club Nautique de L'Esterel) that gives lessons to anyone over age eight.

Biking Bikes can be rented from train stations at **Antibes, Cannes, Juan-les-Pins,** and **Nice.** Two especially scenic trips on fairly level ground are from Nice to the area around Cap d'Antibes and around Cap Ferrat from Cannes. Bikes are ideal at St-Tropez, since the beach is a few miles from town.

Golf There are 18-hole courses at **Cannes, La Napoule, Menton,** and **Monte Carlo** (the last is spectacularly sited on the slopes of Mont Angel).

Horseback Riding Just a couple of miles inland from Mandelieu-La Napoule on N7 is the **Poney Club** (Domaine de Barbossi); children will enjoy the small zoo, as well as the pony rides, while adults can rent horses and, if they like, receive lessons.

Water Sports If you want to get in some sailing while on the Riviera, try **Sportmer** (8 pl. Blanqui) in St-Tropez, and **Yacht Club de Cannes** (Palm Beach Port) and **Camper & Nicholson's** (Port Canto) in Cannes. This is a great area for windsurfing; you can rent equipment from **Le Club Nautique La Croisette** (plage Jardin Pierre-Longue, Cannes), **Centre Nautique Municipal** (9 rue Esprit-Violet, Cannes), and **Sillages** (av. Henry-Clews, Mandelieu-La Napoule).

Beaches

If you like your beaches sandy, stick to those between St-Tropez and Antibes; most of the others are pebbly, though Menton and Monaco have imported vast tons of sand to spread around their shores. Private beaches are everywhere. You'll have to pay to use them (between 80 and 140 francs a day), but you get value for the money—a café or restaurant, cabanas and showers, mattresses and umbrellas, and the pleasure of watching the perpetual parade of stylish swimwear and languid egos.

St-Tropez's best beaches are scattered along a 3-mile stretch reached by the Routes des Plages; the most fashionable are **Moorea, Tahiti Plage,** and **Club 55.** You'll see lots of topless bathers, and some beaches allow total nudity. If you're traveling with children, try the family beaches at **Ste-Maxime** and **St-Raphaël. La Napoule** has no fewer than eight beaches, offering facilities for waterskiing, windsurfing, diving, and snorkeling, or you can just swim or stretch out on a lounge chair. One of Cannes's most fashionable beaches, which belongs to the **Carlton Hotel** and is open from March to October, has a glassed-in terrace and heating to offset out-of-season chills. Nice's beaches extend along the Baie des Anges (the Bay of Angels); **Ruhl Plage** is one of the most popular, with a good restaurant and facilities for waterskiing, windsurfing, and children's swimming lessons. Not to be outdone, **Neptune Plage** has all that plus a sauna.

Dining and Lodging

Dining

Though prices often scale Parisian heights, the Riviera shares its cuisine with Provence, enjoying the same vegetable and fish dishes prepared with vivid seasonings. The most famous is *bouillabaisse*, a fish stew from around Marseille. Genuine bouillabaisse combines *rascasse* (scorpion fish), eel, and half a dozen other types of seafood; crab and lobster are optional. Local fish is scarce, however, so dishes like *loup flambé* (sea bass with fennel and anise liqueur), braised tuna, and even fresh sardines are priced accordingly.

With Italy so close, it's no surprise that many menus feature such specialties as ravioli and potato gnocchi. Try vegetable *soupe au pistou*, an aromatic brew seasoned with basil, garlic, olive oil, and Parmesan cheese, or *pissaladière*, a pastry-based version of pizza, topped with tomato, olives, anchovy, and plenty of onion. Nice claims its own specialties: *pan bagna* (salad in a bun) and *poulpe à la niçoise* (octopus in a tomato sauce). Of the various vegetable dishes, the best is *ratatouille*, a stew of tomatoes, onions, eggplant, and zucchini.

Anise-flavored *pastis* is the Riviera's number-one drink.

Highly recommended restaurants are indicated by a star ★ .

Category	Cost*
Very Expensive	over 500 francs
Expensive	250–500 francs
Moderate	150–250 francs
Inexpensive	under 150 francs

*per person for a three-course meal, including tax (18.6%) and tip but not wine

Lodging

Hotels on the Riviera can push opulence to the sublime—or the ridiculous. Pastel colors, gilt, and plush are the decorators' staple tools in the resort hotels catering to *le beau monde*. The glamour comes hand in hand with hefty price tags, however, and while inexpensive hotels do exist, they're found mainly on the duller outskirts of the big centers and in less fashionable "family" resorts.

Highly recommended hotels are indicated by a star ★ .

Category	Cost*
Very Expensive	over 1,000 francs
Expensive	600–1,000 francs
Moderate	300–600 francs
Inexpensive	under 300 francs

All prices are for a standard double room for two, including tax (18.6%) and service charge.

Antibes
Juan-les-Pins
Dining
★

Bacon. This is the Riviera's top spot for bouillabaisse or any other dish that depends on prime fish, simply and perfectly cooked. The Sordello brothers have run Bacon for over 40 years and don't regard a fish as fresh unless it's still twitching— count on eating only the pick of the local catch. Eat outside on the airy terrace overlooking the port. *Blvd. de Bacon, Cap d'Antibes, tel. 93–61–50–02. Reservations required. Jacket and tie required. AE, DC, MC, V. Closed Sun. dinner, Mon., and mid-Nov.–Jan. Expensive.*

La Bonne Auberge. Chef Jo Rostang and his son Philippe rarely disappoint, with such specialties as lobster ravioli, salads of red mullet, and airy soufflés. The dining room is a flower-filled haven of exposed beams, dim lantern lighting, and rose-colored walls; huge glass windows allow diners a view of the inspired work going on in the kitchen. *Quartier de la Brague, Antibes, tel. 93–33–36–65. Reservations strongly advised. Jacket and tie required. AE, MC, V. Closed Mon. (except for dinner mid-Apr.–Sept.), Wed. lunch (July–Aug.), and mid-Nov.–mid-Dec. Expensive.*

Auberge de l'Esterel. The affable Denis Latouche runs the best moderately priced restaurant in Juan-les-Pins, lending a nouvelle twist to local dishes; try the monkfish and, for dessert, the lemon tart. The secluded garden is a romantic setting for dinner under the stars. There are 15 bedrooms in the small attached hotel. *21 rue des Iles, Juan-les-Pins, tel. 93–61–86–55. Reservations advised. Dress: neat but casual. MC, V. Closed mid-Nov.–mid-Dec., part of Feb., Sun. dinner, and Mon. Moderate–Expensive.*

Dining and Lodging

Grand Hôtel du Cap. Crystal chandeliers, gilt mirrors, gleaming antique furniture, and lots of marble make the Cap d'Antibes a glorious testimony to the opulence of another age. Guest rooms are enormous and feature the same impressive decor as the public rooms. The glass-fronted Pavillon Eden Roc is the place for lobster thermidor, accompanied by vintage champagne. *Blvd. Kennedy, 06600 Antibes, tel. 93–61–39–01. 112 rooms with bath. Facilities: restaurant, tennis, pool. Closed mid-Oct.–Apr. No credit cards. Very Expensive.*

Juana. This luxuriously renovated '30s hotel sits opposite the casino, just a couple of blocks from the beach. Towering pine trees overhang the grounds and the white marble pool. The restaurant, La Terrasse, is one of the best on the Côte d'Azur; chef

Christian Morisset wins praise for his fine seafood creations. Eat outside on the terrace, overlooking the palm trees in the landscaped garden. All the guest rooms are large and individually decorated. *Av. Gallice, 06160 Juan-les-Pins, tel. 93–61–08–70. 45 rooms with bath. Facilities: restaurant, bar, pool. No credit cards. Closed late Oct.–mid-Apr. Very Expensive.*

Djoliba. There are only 14 rooms at this converted Provençal farmhouse, all with a country-house feel. The salon features an airy bamboo-shoot motif, while the guest rooms, painted in a range of pastel shades, have antique furnishings. Choose between views of the park or the sea. The restaurant is open for dinner only. *29 av. de Provence, 06600 Antibes, tel. 93–34–02–48. 14 rooms with bath. Facilities: restaurant, garden, pool. AE, DC, MC, V. Closed Jan.; restaurant closed Oct.–Mar. Moderate.*

Cannes
Dining
★

La Mère Besson. Mix with the locals at this boisterous family eatery that features a range of authentic Provençal fare. Go on Friday for the *aïoli*, a heaped platter of fish, seafood, and boiled vegetables in a thick garlic mayonnaise. The decor borders on the frumpy, but the food is what counts here. *13 rue des Frères-Pradignac, tel. 93–39–59–24. Reservations advised. Dress: casual. AE, DC, MC, V. Closed Sun. except July–Aug. Expensive.*

Villa Dionysos. Thanks to an exceptionally accommodating staff and the dining room's tongue-in-cheek Italianate decor, Villa Dionysos has forged a substantial reputation in the few years since it opened. Dine in the 18th-century Venetian-style dining room or outside on the spectacular terrace. Try the fillet of duck with tarragon sauce or the roast pigeon. *7 rue Marceau, tel. 93–38–79–73. Reservations advised. Dress: neat but casual. AE, MC, V. Moderate–Expensive.*

Au Bec Fin. A devoted band of regulars will attest to the quality of this family-run restaurant near the train station. Don't look for carefully staged decor: It's the spirited local clientele and the homey food that distinguish this cheerful bistro. The fixed-price menus are a fantastic value at 75 or 95 francs; try the fish cooked with fennel or the *salade niçoise*. *12 rue du 24-Août, tel. 93–38–35–86. Reservations advised. Dress: casual. AE, DC, MC, V. Closed Sat. dinner, Sun., and Christmas–late Jan. Inexpensive.*

Lodging
★

Le Fouquet's. If you're looking for a central and comfortable base from which to explore the beach, the shops, the bistros, and the nightclubs, this is the place, located in a quiet residential area of town. The hotel ambience is welcoming—from the entrance, with its brightly lit archway, plants, and mirrors, to the rooms, decorated in warm shades and decked out with lots of French flounces. All the guest rooms are large and feature covered loggias. There's no restaurant. *2 rond-point Duboys-d'Angers, 06400, tel. 93–38–75–81. 10 rooms with bath. AE, DC, MC, V. Closed Nov.–Dec. Expensive.*

Mondial. A three-minute walk from the beach takes you to this six-story hotel, a haven for the traveler seeking solid, unpretentious lodging in a town that tends to lean toward tinsel. Many guest rooms offer sea views. There's no restaurant. *77 rue d'Antibes, 06400, tel. 93–68–70–00. No credit cards. Closed Nov. Moderate.*

Bristol. Halfway between the train station and La Croisette, this hotel probably offers the best value in central Cannes. The quieter rooms (some with small balconies) are at the back. *14* *rue Hoche, 06400, tel. 93–39–10–66. 19 rooms, 15 with shower. Closed Dec. and first half of Jan. AE, MC, V. Inexpensive.*

Dining and Lodging **Carlton.** Cannes's most elegantly old-fashioned hotel is the gleaming white Carlton, built at the turn of the century right on the seafront. The opulent public rooms feature marble floors, chandeliers, floral bouquets, and glittering mirrors. The service, though, is not what it was, and some rooms are cramped. Those in the west wing are best; they're quieter and have terrific views. There are two restaurants: La Côte serves haute cuisine in an imposingly formal atmosphere; the Grill Room is simpler but still impressive. The bar is one of *the* places for mingling with the Riviera's Beautiful People. *58 La Croisette, 06400, tel. 93–68–91–68. 325 rooms with bath. Facilities: restaurants, bar, terrace, health center, private beach. Main restaurant closed Tues., Wed., and Nov.–Christmas. AE, DC, MC, V. Very Expensive.*

Gray d'Albion. This striking contemporary hotel is the last word in state-of-the-art luxury. Its white facade is austere; inside, the atmosphere is ultrasophisticated, with gray and cream walls and plenty of leather, metal, and mirrors. The guest rooms are fitted with slick, modern accessories. There are a number of restaurants; the Royal Gray is one of Cannes's most fashionable. *38 rue des Serbes, 06400, tel. 92–99–79–79. 174 rooms with bath. Facilities: 3 restaurants, disco, private beach. AE, DC, MC, V. Restaurant closed Feb., Sun., and Mon. Very Expensive.*

★ **Martinez.** While many of the luxury palace-hotels that cosseted kings and heads of state have receded into history, the Martinez still manages to retain that sybaritic atmosphere of indulgence, despite the fact it wasn't built until the 1920s—a little late for classic status. The Concorde group bought it in 1982 and revamped it in '30s style, while a gentle renovation in 1989 redid 100 bedrooms in cool blue and salmon shades, with wooden furniture and large marble bathrooms. One of the hotel's biggest assets is the Palme d'Or restaurant, whose chef, Christian Willer, draws lavish praise for his choice line of modern cuisine. *73 La Croisette, 06400, tel. 92–98–73–00. 430 rooms with bath. Facilities: 3 restaurants, tennis, pool, beach, bar. Restaurants closed mid-Nov.–mid-Jan., Feb., and Mon. and Tues. lunch. AE, DC, MC, V. Very Expensive.*

Eze **Château de la Chèvre d'Or.** Located above Monte Carlo in the
Dining and Lodging medieval hilltop village of Eze, the Chèvre d'Or is comprised of
★ a number of ancient houses whose mellow stone walls are set off by terra-cotta pots brimming with geraniums. The guest rooms, though small, are individually decorated and feature antique furnishings and attractive fabrics and wallpapers; ask for room No. 9. The views of Cap Ferrat from the poolside terrace are sensational. The restaurant is dignified, a far cry from some of the Riviera's flashier dining rooms; try the grilled mullet. *Rue du Barri, 06360, tel. 93–41–12–12. 15 rooms with bath. Facilities: restaurant, café, bar, terrace, pool. AE, DC, MC, V. Closed Dec.–Feb. Very Expensive.*

Grasse **Panorama.** This tidy modern hotel has a pleasant, helpful staff
Lodging and well-appointed, soundproof, air-conditioned rooms, where snacks can be served on request. *2 pl. Cours, 06130, tel. 93–36–80–80. 36 rooms with bath. MC, V. Moderate.*

La Napoule **Le Domaine d'Olival.** There's not the slightest hint of mass
Lodging production at this charming hotel, whose rooms have been in-

dividually designed by the architect-owner. It's small, so make reservations long in advance. All the guest rooms are air-conditioned and have balconies, as well as tiny kitchens. Some suites sleep six, which brings the price per couple down to Moderate. *778 av. de la Mer, 06210, tel. 93–49–31–00. 18 rooms with bath. AE, DC, MC, V. Closed Nov.–mid-Jan. Expensive.*

Dining and Lodging **Royal Hôtel Casino.** Weighing in at just over 200 rooms, this is a pocket edition of the Loews at Monte Carlo, with plenty of marble, plush, and gilt. The guest rooms have sea views and balconies and are decorated in pink and blue, with blond wooden furniture and large bathrooms. Be warned: Rooms overlooking the main road can be noisy. Diners at the moderately priced restaurant can gaze out over a flood-lit swimming pool and deliberate among such textbook delicacies as caviar, lobster, and vintage champagne; try the grilled fish. *Blvd. Henry-Clews, 06210, tel. 93–49–90–00. 211 rooms with bath. Facilities: pool, casino, restaurants, cabaret, bars, shops, bank, travel agency, tennis. AE, DC, MC, V. Expensive.*

Menton **Auberge des Santons.** Sea views and a peaceful setting on a hill
Dining and Lodging near l'Annonciade Monastery are the lures of this tiny hotel. The spacious white villa has studio apartments for longer stays. The British owners have studied the art of Oriental cooking, so restaurant specials range from a traditional Chinese banquet to mince pie to Provençal dishes. *Colline de l'Annonciade, 06500, tel. 93–35–94–10. 9 rooms with bath. Facilities: restaurant. AE, MC, V. Moderate.*

Londres. This small, central hotel, close to the beach and casino, has its own restaurant, serving solid, traditional French cuisine, and a small garden for outdoor summer dining. *15 av. Carnot, 06500, tel. 93–35–74–62. 26 rooms with shower or bath. Facilities: restaurant (closed Wed.), bar, ping-pong. AE, MC, V. Inexpensive–Moderate.*

Monte Carlo **Port.** Harbor views from the terrace and top-notch Italian food
Dining make the Port a good choice. A large, varied menu includes shrimp, pastas, lasagna, fettuccine, fish risotto, and veal with ham and cheese. *Quai Albert Ier, tel. 93–50–77–21. Reservations advised. Dress: casual. AE, DC, MC, V. Closed Mon. and Nov. Moderate–Expensive.*

★ **Polpetta.** This popular little trattoria is close enough to the Italian border to pass for the real McCoy and is excellent value for the money. If it's on the menu, go for the vegetable *soupe au pistou. 2 rue Paradis, tel. 93–50–67–84. Reservations required in summer. Dress: casual. V. Closed Tues. and Sat. lunch and Feb. Inexpensive–Moderate.*

Lodging **Alexandra.** Shades of the Belle Epoque linger in this comfortable hotel's spacious lobby and airy guest rooms. Tan and rose colors dominate the newer rooms. If you're willing to do without a private bath, this place sneaks into the Inexpensive category. The friendly proprietress, Madame Larouquie, makes foreign visitors feel right at home. *35 blvd. Princesse-Charlotte, 98000, tel. 93–50–63–13. 55 rooms, 46 with bath. AE, DC, MC, V. Moderate.*

Dining and Lodging **Hôtel de Paris.** Though discreetly modernized, the Hôtel de
★ Paris still exudes the gold-plated splendor of an era in which kings and granddukes stayed here. The restaurant, the Louis XV, stuns you with such royal decor that you may be distracted from the food, but make the effort to give it your attention,

since Alain Ducasse is one of Europe's most celebrated chefs. Try his ravioli de foie gras. *Pl. du Casino, 98000, tel. 93–50–80–80. 255 rooms with bath. Restaurant closed Tues., Wed. (except dinner July–Aug.), late Feb.–early Mar., and Nov.–Dec. Very Expensive.*

Loews. Big, brash, and more than a touch vulgar, Loews has a plush extravagance on a scale Donald Trump would envy. Fountains splash, contemporary rooms are decorated in ice-cream shades, and celebrities mix with sheikhs in the bars, casino, and restaurants. Die-hard football fans can watch the Super Bowl by satellite; those in search of live entertainment should head for the Folie Russe, boasting lines of scantily clad showgirls and mountains of caviar. *12 av. des Spélugues, 98000, tel. 93–50–65–00. 650 rooms with bath. Facilities: restaurants, pool, health spa, casino, Jacuzzi. AE, DC, MC, V. Very Expensive.*

Mougins
Dining and Lodging
★

Moulin de Mougins. A 16th-century olive mill houses one of the country's top 20 restaurants. Chef Roger Vergé has an ever-changing repertoire and creates new dishes every season. Some of them capitalize on traditional regional cuisine; others are innovative concoctions using lobster, caviar, and other ingredients that many crave but few can afford. The intimate beamed dining rooms, with oil paintings, plants, and porcelain tableware, are the perfect setting for world-class fare. In summer, dine outside under the awnings. There are five elegantly rustic guest rooms as well. *Notre-Dame-de-Vie, 06250, tel. 93–75–78–24. Reservations required. Jacket and tie required. AE, DC, MC, V. Closed Feb.–Mar., Mon. (except summer), and Thurs. lunch (times are variable). Very Expensive.*

Nice
Dining
★

Ane Rouge. The Vidalots run a tight ship. Their tiny restaurant, perched right by the harbor, is always crowded and has been famous for generations as the place to go to for Nice's best fish and seafood. Best bets are the sea bass braised in champagne and the stuffed mussels. *7 quai des Deux-Emmanuel, tel. 93–89–49–63. Reservations advised. Dress: neat but casual. AE, DC, MC, V. Closed Sat., Sun., and mid-July–Sept. Very Expensive.*

★

La Mérenda. This noisy bistro lies in the heart of the old town, and its down-to-earth Italo-Provençal food is tremendously good value. The Giustis, who run it, refuse to install a telephone, so go early to be sure of getting a table. House specials include pasta with *pistou* (a garlic-and-basil sauce) and succulent tripe. *4 rue de la Terrasse. No reservations. Dress: casual. No credit cards. Closed Sat., Sun., Mon., Feb., and Aug. Moderate.*

L'Olivier. Franck Musso bakes his own bread and serves up sturdy Provençal dishes (fish soup, snail ravioli) and homemade desserts, while his brother Christian provides guests with a chirpy welcome to the small, cozy dining room lined with pictures. Locals love it, and because the restaurant seats only 20, book ahead. *2 pl. Garibaldi, tel. 93–26–89–09. Reservations required. Dress: casual. AE, MC, V. Closed Sun., Mon. lunch, and most of Aug. and Dec. Moderate.*

Lodging

Little Palace. Monsieur and Madame Loridan run the closest thing to a country-house hotel in Nice. The old-fashioned decor, the jumble of bric-a-brac, and the heavy wooden furniture lend an Old World air; some may say it's like stepping onto a film set. *9 av. Baquis, 06000, tel. 93–88–70–49. 36 rooms, 31 with bath. MC, V. Closed Nov. Inexpensive.*

La Mer. This small hotel is handily situated on place Masséna, close to the old town and seafront. The rooms are spartan (and carpets are sometimes frayed), but all have a minibar and represent good value. Ask for a room away from the square to be sure of a quiet night. *4 pl. Masséna, 06000, tel. 93–92–09–10. 12 rooms with bath or shower. No credit cards. Inexpensive.*

Dining and Lodging **Elysée Palace.** This glass-fronted addition to the Nice hotel scene lies close to the seafront; all guest rooms feature views of the Mediterranean. The interior is spacious and ultramodern, with plenty of marble in evidence. The large restaurant is a sound bet for nouvelle cuisine, enjoyed amid surroundings of contemporary works of art. *59 promenade des Anglais, 06000, tel. 93–86–06–06. 143 rooms with bath. Facilities: restaurant, pool, sauna, health club, bar, AE, DC, MC, V. Very Expensive.*

★ **Negresco.** Henri Negresco wanted to out-Ritz all the Ritzes when he built this place. There were eight kings at the opening ceremony in 1912, grouped on the 560,000-franc gold Aubusson carpet (the world's largest, naturally) beneath the one-ton crystal chandelier in the great oval salon. No two rooms are the same (except for the bathroom fittings), though all feature antique furniture and classical decor, evocative of various periods from the 16th through the 19th centuries. Chef Dominique le Stanc forged a name for himself in Monte Carlo and is consolidating the Chantecler restaurant's reputation as one of France's finest dining rooms. *37 promenade des Anglais, 06000, tel. 93–88–39–51. 130 rooms with bath. Facilities: 2 restaurants, bar, private beach. Very Expensive.*

★ **Beau Rivage.** Occupying an imposing late-19th-century town house near the cours Saleya, the Beau Rivage is run by the same hotel group (Clef d'Or) as the Elysée Palace (*see above*). Though the rooms are decorated in a similar modern style, the overall effect is more intimate and personal here. Renowned chef Roger Vergé oversees a catering school on the premises; his nouvelle touch can be appreciated in the hotel's fine restaurant. *24 rue St-François-de-Paule, 06000, tel. 93–80–80–70. 110 rooms with bath. Facilities: restaurant, private beach. AE, DC, MC, V. Expensive–Very Expensive.*

St-Paul-de-Vence **Colombe d'Or.** Anyone who likes the ambience of a country inn
Dining and Lodging will feel right at home here. You'll be paying for your room or
★ meal with cash or credit cards; Picasso, Klee, Dufy, Utrillo—all friends of the former owner—paid with the paintings that now decorate the walls. The restaurant has a very good reputation. The Colombe d'Or is certainly on the tourist trail, but many of the tourists who stay here are rich and famous—if that's any consolation. *Pl. Général-de-Gaulle, 06570 St-Paul-de-Vence, tel. 93–32–80–02. 24 rooms with bath. Facilities: restaurant, pool. AE, DC, MC, V. Closed mid-Nov.–late Dec., part of Jan. Expensive.*

St-Tropez **Bistrot des Lices.** You'll find a mix of celebrities and locals at
Dining this popular bistro, a hot spot for interesting food, served by a staff as fashionable as the clientele. Bronzed men and glamorous women lounge in the garden or eat inside in the pastel interior. The barman is renowned for his way with a cocktail shaker, high praise in a town where cocktails are a way of life. *3 pl. des Lices, tel. 94–97–29–00. Reservations advised. Dress:*

neat but casual. *MC, V. Closed Tues. out of season and Jan.–
Mar. Moderate.*

Le Girelier. Fish enthusiasts—especially those with a taste for
garlic—will enjoy the hearty, heavily spiced dishes at this bustling restaurant, located right on the quay. The fish soup and
the giant shrimp are local favorites. *Quai Jean-Jaurès, tel. 94–
97–03–87. Reservations accepted. Dress: casual. AE, DC,
MC, V. Closed mid-Jan.–early Mar. Moderate.*

Lodging **Ermitage.** This is the ideal town hotel, featuring an old-
fashioned charm rarely found in modern-day St-Tropez. The
guest rooms' white walls are offset by coordinated patterns of
strong primary colors on the beds and at the windows. There's
no restaurant. *Av. Paul-Signac, 83990, tel. 94–97–52–33. 27
rooms with bath. AE, DC, MC, V. Expensive.*

Lou Cagnard. This is one of the few inexpensive hotels in St-
Tropez, just two minutes' walk from place des Lices, so book
well ahead. Don't expect great style or comfort, but the rooms
are clean and not too cramped. *18 av. Paul-Roussel, 83990, tel.
94–97–04–24. 19 rooms, most with bath or shower. No credit
cards. Closed Nov.–Christmas. Inexpensive.*

Dining and Lodging **Byblos.** The Byblos is the Côte d'Azur's sophisticated answer to
Disneyland. Designed with ingenuity, taste, and humor, the
complex resembles a Provençal village, with cottagelike suites
grouped around courtyards paved with Picasso-inspired tiles
and shaded by olive trees and magnolias. Inside, the atmosphere is distinctly New York Casbah, with lots of heavy dam-
ask and hammered brass, a leopard-skin bar, and Persian
carpets on the dining-room ceiling. If you can't afford to stay
here, at least go to use the pool (for a steep fee). The restaurant, Le Chabichou, is lucky to have the talented Michel
Rochedy as chef; his grilled sardines are memorable. *Av. Paul
Signac, 83990, tel. 94–97–00–04. 106 rooms with bath. Facilities: restaurant, pool, nightclub. AE, DC, MC, V. Closed
Nov.–Feb. Very Expensive.*

Le Mas de Chastelas. In an old farmhouse that was once a silkworm farm, guests can enjoy a happy marriage of traditional
and modern surroundings. The pink-toned facade, offset by
white shutters, is half hidden behind trees and flowering
shrubbery. Inside, white walls, modern furniture, and sculptures by the owner's sister combine to create a cool retreat
from the blazing Mediterranean sun. The restaurant is usually
filled with a congenial mélange of celebrities and well-heeled
travelers, attracted by the subtle cuisine (asparagus with sea
urchins, for example) of chef Michel Gaudin. *Rte. de Gassin,
83990, tel. 94–56–09–11. 30 rooms with bath. Facilities: restaurant, pool. AE, DC, MC, V. Closed Nov.–Easter. Very Expensive.*

Vence **Château St-Martin.** The secluded, elite St-Martin stands on the
Dining and Lodging site of a crusader castle, surrounded by tall, shady trees and
★ set within spacious grounds. The guest rooms are exquisitely
decorated with antiques, needlepoint, and brocade; those in
the tower are smaller and less expensive but feature the same
loving attention to detail. There's an excellent restaurant serving Provençal-inspired dishes. *Rte. de Coursegoules, 06140,
tel. 93–58–02–02. 25 rooms with bath. Facilities: restaurant,
garden, pool, tennis, helicopter landing pad. AE, DC, MC, V.
Closed mid-Nov.–mid.-Mar. Very Expensive.*

La Roseraie. While there's no rose garden here, a giant magno-

lia spreads its venerable branches over the terrace. Chef Maurice Ganier hails from the southwest, as do the ducks that form
the basis of his cooking. Polished service and sophisticated
menus prove that you don't have to be rich to enjoy life in this
part of France. There are 12 guest rooms and a swimming pool.
*51 av. Henri-Giraud, 06140, tel. 93–58–02–20. 12 rooms with
bath. Facilities: restaurant, pool. AE, MC, V. Closed Jan.;
restaurant closed Tues. lunch and Wed. Moderate.*

The Arts and Nightlife

The Arts

Festivals The Riviera's cultural calendar is splashy and star-studded,
and never more so than during the region's world-famous festivals. The biggest and most celebrated is the **Cannes Film Festival** in May, rivaled by Monte Carlo's arts festival, **Printemps
des Arts** (late March through late April). Antibes and Nice both
host **jazz festivals** during July, drawing international performers. Menton has a **chamber music festival** in August and a **September music festival** at the Palais d'Europe.

Music and Ballet Monte Carlo's primary venue for jazz and rock is **Le Chapiteau
de Fontvieille** (tel. 93–25–18–68); the **Salle Garnier** (Casino de
Monaco, tel. 93–50–76–54) offers both classical music and ballet, as does Nice's **Acropolis** (Palais des Congrès, Esplanade,
John F. Kennedy, tel. 93–92–80–80). St-Tropez's major con-
cert hall is the **Salle de la Renaissance** (pl. des Lices, tel. 94–97–
48–16). There are frequent jazz and pop concerts at Nice's **Théâtre de Verdure** (Jardin Albert Ier, tel. 93–82–38–68), which re-
locates to the **Arènes de Cimiez** during summer months.

Opera The Nice **Opéra** (4 rue St-François-de-Paul, tel. 93–85–67–31)
has a season that extends from September to June. In Monte
Carlo, the **Salle Garnier** (*see* above) hosts operatic performances, most frequently during the spring arts festival.

Theater In Nice try the **Théâtre Municipal du Vieux-Nice** (4 rue St-Jo-
seph, tel. 93–62–00–03) or the **Café-Théâtre de Nice** (12 av. St-
Jean-Baptiste, tel. 93–85–40–28). In Monte Carlo, the **Théâtre
Princesse Grace** (12 av. d'Ostende, tel. 93–25–32–27) stages a
number of plays during the spring festival; off-season, there's
usually a new show each week.

Nightlife

There's no need to go to bed before dawn in any of the Riviera's
major resorts, the most fashionable of which are St-Tropez,
Cannes, Juan-les-Pins, Nice, and Monte Carlo. Juan-les-Pins
draws a young crowd; St-Tropez has gay appeal; and clubs in
Cannes, Nice, and Monte Carlo are expensive and sophisticated. Note that to get into many of the Riviera's night spots,
you'll have to dress the part—or risk being brushed aside by
the burly doormen.

Discos and La Siesta (rte. du Bord de Mer, Antibes) is an enormous setup,
Nightclubs with seven dance floors, roulette, bars, and supper places—all
dramatically lit by torches; it's open during the summer season
only. The top spot in Cannes is the **Studio-Circus** (52 blvd. de la
République), which admits celebrities, stars, and starlets, but
not necessarily everyone else. The cabaret shows are legen-

dary, accompanied by lasers and deafening noise. Top-class cabaret is offered at Menton's **Club 06,** at the casino (Promenade de Soleil). In Monte Carlo, head to **Jimmy'z;** it operates from place du Casino from September to June, then moves to premises on avenue Princesse-Grace (at No. 26). The location may be different, but the disco remains expensive and chic, and the clientele is drawn from the elite. The **Spirit** (plage du Larvotto) is a friendly place whose devotees dance from 11:30 PM to dawn all year (closed Mon.). In the avenue des Spélugues, you'll find **The Living Room** (at No. 7) and **Tiffany's** (at No. 3); both are popular, crowded, and open year-round. **The Offshore** (29 rue Alphonse-Karr) is Nice's trendiest spot, but you'll have to dress sharp to get past the doorman. If you don't make it, try the young, lively **Bin's Discothèque** (71 blvd. Jean-Béhra). The hottest place in St-Tropez is **Les Caves du Roy** (Byblos Hotel, av. Signac); the decor is stunningly vulgar, but the *très chic* clientele don't seem to mind. It's large but always crowded, so look your best if you want to get in.

Casinos   There are casinos in **Cannes** (pl. Franklin-Roosevelt), **Nice** (Promenade des Anglais), and **Menton** (Promenade de Soleil), but the Riviera's most famous gambling venue is at **Monte Carlo** (pl. du Casino).

Conversion Tables

Distance

Kilometers/Miles To change kilometers to miles, multiply kilometers by .621
To change miles to kilometers, multiply miles by 1.61

Km to Mi	Mi to Km
1 = .62	1 = 1.6
2 = 1.2	2 = 3.2
3 = 1.9	3 = 4.8
4 = 2.5	4 = 6.4
5 = 3.1	5 = 8.1
6 = 3.7	6 = 9.7
7 = 4.3	7 = 11.3
8 = 5.0	8 = 12.9
9 = 5.6	9 = 14.5

Meters/Feet To change meters to feet, multiply meters by 3.28
To change feet to meters, multiply feet by .305

Meters to Feet	Feet to Meters
1 = 3.3	1 = .31
2 = 6.6	2 = .61
3 = 9.8	3 = .92
4 = 13.1	4 = 1.2
5 = 16.4	5 = 1.5
6 = 19.7	6 = 1.8
7 = 23.0	7 = 2.1
8 = 26.2	8 = 2.4
9 = 29.5	9 = 2.7

Weight

Kilograms/Pounds To change kilograms to pounds, multiply by 2.20
To change pounds to kilograms, multiply by .453

Kilos to Pounds	Pounds to Kilos
1 = 2.2	1 = .45
2 = 4.4	2 = .91
3 = 6.6	3 = 1.4
4 = 8.8	4 = 1.8
5 = 11.0	5 = 2.3

6 = 13.2	6 = 2.7
7 = 15.4	7 = 3.2
8 = 17.6	8 = 3.6
9 = 19.8	9 = 4.1

Grams/Ounces To change grams to ounces, multiply grams by .035
To change ounces to grams, multiply ounces by 28.4

Grams to Ounces	Ounces to Grams
1 = .04	1 = 28
2 = .07	2 = 57
3 = .11	3 = 85
4 = .14	4 = 114
5 = .18	5 = 142
6 = .21	6 = 170
7 = .25	7 = 199
8 = .28	8 = 227
9 = .32	9 = 256

Liquid Volume

Liters/U.S. Gallons To change liters to U.S. gallons, multiply liters by .264
To change U.S. gallons to liters, multiply gallons by 3.79

Liters to U.S. Gallons	U.S. Gallons to Liters
1 = .26	1 = 3.8
2 = .53	2 = 7.6
3 = .79	3 = 11.4
4 = 1.1	4 = 15.2
5 = 1.3	5 = 19.0
6 = 1.6	6 = 22.7
7 = 1.8	7 = 26.5
8 = 2.1	8 = 30.3
9 = 2.4	9 = 34.1

Clothing Sizes

Men To change American suit sizes to French suit sizes, add 10 to
Suits the American suit size.

To change French suit sizes to American suit sizes, subtract 10
from the French suit size.

U.S.	36	38	40	42	44	46	48
French	46	48	50	52	54	56	58

Shirts To change American shirt sizes to French shirt sizes, multiply the American shirt size by 2 and add 8.

To change French shirt sizes to American shirt sizes, subtract 8 from the French shirt size and divide by 2.

U.S.	14	14½	15	15½	16	16½	17	17½
French	36	37	38	39	40	41	42	43

Shoes French shoe sizes vary in their relation to American shoe sizes.

U.S.	6½	7	8	9	10	10½	11
French	39	40	41	42	43	44	45

Women
Dresses and Coats To change U.S. dress/coat sizes to French dress/coat sizes, add 28 to the U.S. dress/coat size.

To change French dress/coat sizes to U.S. dress/coat sizes, subtract 28 from the French dress/coat size.

U.S.	4	6	8	10	12	14	16
French	32	34	36	38	40	42	44

Blouses and Sweaters To change U.S. blouse/sweater sizes to French blouse/sweater sizes, add 8 to the U.S. blouse/sweater size.

To change French blouse/sweater sizes to U.S. blouse/sweater sizes, subtract 8 from the French blouse/sweater size.

U.S.	30	32	34	36	38	40	42
French	38	40	42	44	46	48	50

Shoes To change U.S. shoe sizes to French shoe sizes, add 32 to the U.S. shoe size.

To change French shoe sizes to U.S. shoe sizes, subtract 32 from the French shoe size.

U.S.	4	5	6	7	8	9	10
French	36	37	38	39	40	41	42

French Vocabulary

Words and Phrases

	English	*French*	*Pronunciation*
Basics	Yes/no	Oui/non	wee/no
	Please	S'il vous plaît	seel voo play
	Thank you	Merci	mare-**see**
	You're welcome	De rien	deh ree-**en**
	Excuse me, sorry	Pardon	pahr-**doan**
	Sorry!	Désolé(e)	day-zoh-**lay**
	Good morning/ afternoon	Bonjour	bone-**joor**
	Good evening	Bonsoir	bone-**swar**
	Goodbye	Au revoir	o ruh-**vwar**
	Mr. (Sir)	Monsieur	mih-see-**oor**
	Mrs. (Ma'am)	Madame	ma-dam
	Miss	Mademoiselle	mad-mwa-**zel**
	Pleased to meet you	Enchanté(e)	on-shahn-**tay**
	How are you?	Comment allez-vous?	ko-men-tahl-ay-**voo**
Numbers	one	un	un
	two	deux	dew
	three	trois	twa
	four	quatre	**cat**-ruh
	five	cinq	sank
	six	six	seess
	seven	sept	set
	eight	huit	wheat
	nine	neuf	nuf
	ten	dix	deess
	eleven	onze	owns
	twelve	douze	dooz
	thirteen	treize	trays
	fourteen	quatorze	ka-torz
	fifteen	quinze	cans
	sixteen	seize	sez
	seventeen	dix-sept	deess-**set**
	eighteen	dix-huit	deess-**wheat**
	nineteen	dix-neuf	deess-**nuf**
	twenty	vingt	vant
	twenty-one	vingt-et-un	vant-ay-**un**
	thirty	trente	trahnt
	forty	quarante	ka-**rahnt**
	fifty	cinquante	sang-**kahnt**
	sixty	soixante	swa-**sahnt**
	seventy	soixante-dix	swa-sahnt-**deess**
	eighty	quatre-vingts	cat-ruh-**vant**
	ninety	quatre-vingt-dix	cat-ruh-vant-**deess**
	one-hundred	cent	sahnt
	one-thousand	mille	meel
Colors	black	noir	nwar
	blue	bleu	blu

	brown	brun/marron	brun
	green	vert	vair
	orange	orange	o-**ranj**
	red	rouge	rouge
	white	blanc	blahn
	yellow	jaune	jone

Days of the Week	Sunday	dimanche	dee-**mahnsh**
	Monday	lundi	lewn-**dee**
	Tuesday	mardi	mar-**dee**
	Wednesday	mercredi	mare-kruh-**dee**
	Thursday	jeudi	juh-**dee**
	Friday	vendredi	van-dra-**dee**
	Saturday	samedi	sam-**dee**

Months	January	janvier	jan-**vyay**
	February	février	feh-vree-**ay**
	March	mars	marce
	April	avril	a-**vreel**
	May	mai	meh
	June	juin	jwan
	July	juillet	jwee-**ay**
	August	août	oot
	September	septembre	sep-**tahm**-bruh
	October	octobre	oak-**toe**-bruh
	November	novembre	no-**vahm**-bruh
	December	décembre	day-**sahm**-bruh

Useful Phrases	Do you speak English?	Parlez-vous anglais?	par-lay vooz ahng-**glay**
	I don't speak French	Je ne parle pas français	jeh nuh parl pah fraun-**say**
	I don't understand	Je ne comprends pas	jeh nuh kohm-prahn **pah**
	I understand	Je comprends	jeh kohm-**prahn**
	I don't know	Je ne sais pas	jeh nuh say **pah**
	I'm American/ British	Je suis américain/ anglais	jeh sweez a-may-ree-**can**/ahng-**glay**
	What's your name?	Comment vous appelez-vous?	ko-mahn voo za-pel-ay-**voo**
	My name is . . .	Je m'appelle . . .	jeh muh-**pel** . . .
	What time is it?	Quelle heure est-il?	kel ur et-**il**
	How?	Comment?	ko-**mahn**
	When?	Quand?	kahnd
	Yesterday	Hier	yair
	Today	Aujourd'hui	o-zhoor-**dwee**
	Tomorrow	Demain	deh-**man**
	This morning/ afternoon	Ce matin/cet après-midi	seh ma-**tanh**/set ah-pray-mee-**dee**
	Tonight	Ce soir	seh **swar**

What?	Quoi?	kwah
What is it?	Qu'est-ce que c'est?	kess-kuh-**say**
Why?	Pourquoi?	poor-**kwa**
Who?	Qui?	kee
Where is . . .	Où est . . .	oo ay
the train station?	la gare?	la gar
the subway station?	la station de métro?	la sta-syon deh may-**tro**
the bus stop?	l'arrêt de bus?	la-ray deh **booss**
the terminal (airport)?	l'aérogare?	lay-ro-**gar**
the post office?	la poste?	la post
the bank?	la banque?	la bahnk
the . . . hotel?	l'hôtel . . . ?	low-**tel**
the . . . museum?	le musée . . . ?	leh mew-**zay**
the hospital?	l'hôpital?	low-pee-**tahl**
the elevator?	l'ascenseur?	la-sahn-**seur**
the telephone?	le téléphone?	leh te-le-**phone**
Where are the restrooms?	Où sont les toilettes?	oo son lay twah-**let**
Here/there	Ici/lá	ee-**see**/la
Left/right	A gauche/à droite	a goash/a drwat
Is it near/far?	C'est près/loin?	say pray/lwan
I'd like . . .	Je voudrais . . .	jeh voo-**dray**
a room	une chambre	ewn **shahm**-bra
the key	la clé	la clay
a newspaper	un journal	un joor-**nahl**
a stamp	un timbre	un **tam**-bruh
I'd like to buy . . .	Je voudrais acheter . . .	jeh voo-**dray** ahsh-**tay**
cigarettes	des cigarettes	day see-ga-**ret**
matches	des allumettes	days a-loo-**met**
city plan	un plan de ville	un plahn de la **veel**
road map	une carte routière	ewn cart roo-tee-**air**
magazine	une revue	ewn reh-**view**
envelopes	des enveloppes	dayz ahn-veh-**lope**
writing paper	du papier à lettres	deh-pa-pee-ay a **let**-ruh
airmail writing paper	du papier avion	deh pa-pee-ay a-vee-**own**
postcard	une carte postale	ewn cart post-**al**
How much is it?	C'est combien?	say comb-bee-**en**
It's expensive/cheap	C'est cher/pas cher	say sher/pa sher
A little/a lot	Un peu/beaucoup	un puh/bo-**koo**
More/less	Plus/moins	ploo/mwa
Enough/too (much)	Assez/trop	a-**say**/tro

	I am ill/sick	Je suis malade	jeh swee ma-**lahd**
	Call a doctor	Appelez un docteur	a-pe-lay un dohk-**tore**
	Help!	Au secours!	o say-**koor**
	Stop!	Arrêtez!	a-ruh-**tay**
Dining Out	A bottle of . . .	une bouteille de . . .	ewn boo-**tay** deh
	A cup of . . .	une tasse de . . .	ewn tass deh
	A glass of . . .	un verre de . . .	un vair deh
	Ashtray	un cendrier	un sahn-dree-**ay**
	Bill/check	l'addition	la-dee-see-**own**
	Bread	du pain	due pan
	Breakfast	le petit déjeuner	leh pet-**ee** day-zhu-**nay**
	Butter	du beurre	due bur
	Cocktail/aperitif	un apéritif	un ah-pay-ree-**teef**
	Dinner	le dîner	leh dee-**nay**
	Fixed-price menu	le menu	leh may-**new**
	Fork	une fourchette	ewn four-**shet**
	I am on a diet	Je suis au régime	jeh sweez o ray-**jeem**
	I am vegetarian	Je suis végétarien(ne)	jeh swee vay-jay-ta-ree-**en**
	I cannot eat . . .	Je ne peux pas manger de . . .	jeh nuh puh pah mahn-**jay** deh
	I'd like to order	Je voudrais commander	jeh voo-**dray** ko-mahn-**day**
	I'd like . . .	Je voudrais . . .	jeh voo-**dray**
	I'm hungry/thirsty	J'ai faim/soif	jay fam/swahf
	Is service/the tip included?	Est-ce que le service est compris?	ess keh leh sair-veess ay comb-**pree**
	It's good/bad	C'est bon/mauvais	say bon/mo-**vay**
	It's hot/cold	C'est chaud/froid	say sho/frwah
	Knife	un couteau	un koo-**toe**
	Lunch	le déjeuner	leh day-juh-**nay**
	Menu	la carte	la cart
	Napkin	une serviette	ewn sair-vee-**et**
	Pepper	du poivre	due **pwah**-vruh
	Plate	une assiette	ewn a-see-**et**
	Please give me . . .	Donnez-moi . . .	doe-nay-**mwah**
	Salt	du sel	dew sell

Spoon	une cuillère	ewn kwee-**air**
Sugar	du sucre	due **sook**-ruh
Wine list	la carte des vins	la cart day **van**

Menu Guide

English	*French*
Set menu	Menu à prix fixe
Dish of the day	Plat du jour
Drink included	Boisson comprise
Local specialties	Spécialités locales
Choice of vegetable accompaniment	Garniture au choix
Made to order	Sur commande
Extra charge	Supplément/En sus
When available	Selon arrivage

Breakfast

Jam	Confiture
Croissants	Croissants
Honey	Miel
Boiled egg	Oeuf à la coque
Bacon and eggs	Oeufs au bacon
Ham and eggs	Oeufs au jambon
Fried eggs	Oeufs sur le plat
Scrambled eggs	Oeufs brouillés
(Plain) omelet	Omelette (nature)
Rolls	Petits pains

Starters

Anchovies	Anchois
Chitterling sausage	Andouille(tte)
Assorted cold cuts	Assiette anglaise
Assorted pork products	Assiette de charcuterie
Small, highly seasoned sausage	Crépinette
Mixed raw vegetable salad	Crudités
Snails	Escargots
Ham (Bayonne)	Jambon (de Bayonne)
Bologna sausage	Mortadelle
Devilled eggs	Oeufs à la diable
Liver purée blended with other meat	Pâté
Tart with a rich, creamy filling of cheese, vegetables, meat or seafood	Quiche (lorraine)
Cold sausage	Saucisson
Pâté sliced and served from an earthenware pot	Terrine
Cured dried beef	Viande séchée

Salads

Diced vegetable salad	Salade russe
Endive salad	Salade d'endives
Green salad	Salade verte
Mixed salad	Salade panachée
Tuna salad	Salade de thon

Soups

Cold leek and potato cream soup	Vichyssoise
Cream of . . .	Crème de . . .
Cream of . . .	Velouté de . . .
Hearty soup	Soupe
day's soup	*du jour*
French onion soup	à l'oignon
Provençal vegetable soup	au pistou
Light soup	Potage
mashed red beans	*condé*
shredded vegetables	julienne
potato	parmentier
Fish and seafood stew	Bouillabaisse
Seafood stew (chowder)	Bisque
Stew of meat and vegetables	Pot-au-feu

Fish and Seafood

Bass	Bar
Carp	Carpe
Clams	Palourdes
Cod	Morue
Creamed salt cod	Brandade de morue
Crab	Crabe
Crayfish	Ecrevisses
Eel	Anguille
Fish stew from Marseilles	Bourride
Fish stew in wine	Matelote
Frog's legs	Cuisses de grenouilles
Herring	Harengs
Lobster	Homard
Mackerel	Maquereau
Mussels	Moules
Octopus	Poulpe
Oysters	Huîtres
Perch	Perche
Pike	Brochet
Dublin bay prawns (scampi)	Langoustines
Red mullet	Rouget
Salmon	Saumon
Scallops in creamy sauce	Coquilles St-Jacques
Sea bream	Daurade
Shrimps	Crevettes
Sole	Sole
Squid	Calmar
Trout	Truite
Tuna	Thon
Whiting	Merlan

Methods of Preparation

Baked	Au four
Fried	Frit
Grilled	Grillé
Marinated	Mariné
Poached	Poché
Sautéed	Sauté
Smoked	Fumé
Steamed	Cuit à la vapeur

Meat

Beef	Boeuf
Beef stew with vegetables, braised in red Burgundy wine	Boeuf bourguignon
Brains	Cervelle
Chops	Côtelettes
Cutlet	Escalope
Double fillet steak	Chateaubriand
Kabob	Brochette
Kidneys	Rognons
Lamb	Agneau
Leg	Gigot
Liver	Foie
Meatballs	Boulettes de viande
Pig's feet (trotters)	Pieds de cochon
Pork	Porc
Rib	Côte
Rib or rib-eye steak	Entrecôte
Sausages	Saucisses
Sausages and cured pork served with sauerkraut	Choucroute garnie
Steak (always beef)	Steak/steack
Stew	Ragoût
T-bone steak	Côte de boeuf
Tenderloin steak	Médaillon
Tenderloin of T-bone steak	Tournedos
Tongue	Langue
Veal	Veau
Veal sweetbreads	Ris de veau

Methods of Preparation

Very rare	Bleu
Rare	Saignant
Medium	A point
Well-done	Bien cuit
Baked	Au four
Boiled	Bouilli
Braised	Braisé
Fried	Frit
Grilled	Grillé
Roast	Rôti
Sautéed	Sauté
Stewed	A l'étouffée

Game and Poultry

Chicken	Poulet
Chicken breast	Suprême de volaille
Chicken stewed in red wine	Coq au vin
Chicken stewed with vegetables	Poule au pot
Spring chicken	Poussin
Duck/duckling	Canard/caneton
Duck braised with oranges and orange liqueur	Canard à l'orange
Fattened pullet	Poularde
Fowl	Volaille
Guinea fowl/young guinea fowl	Pintade/pintadeau
Goose	Oie

Partridge/young partridge	Perdrix/perdreau
Pheasant	Faisan
Pigeon/squab	Pigeon/pigeonneau
Quail	Caille
Rabbit	Lapin
Turkey/young turkey	Dinde/dindonneau
Venison (red/roe)	Cerf/chevreuil

Vegetables

Artichoke	Artichaut
Asparagus	Asperge
Brussels sprouts	Choux de Bruxelles
Cabbage (red)	Chou (rouge)
Carrots	Carottes
Cauliflower	Chou-fleur
Eggplant	Aubergines
Endive	Endives
Leeks	Poireaux
Lettuce	Laitue
Mushrooms	Champignons
Onions	Oignons
Peas	Petits pois
Peppers	Poivrons
Radishes	Radis
Spinach	Epinards
Tomatoes	Tomates
Watercress	Cresson
Zucchini	Courgette
White kidney/French beans	Haricots blancs/verts
Casserole of stewed eggplant, onions, green peppers, and zucchini	Ratatouille

Spices and Herbs

Bay leaf	Laurier
Chervil	Cerfeuil
Garlic	Ail
Marjoram	Marjolaine
Mustard	Moutarde
Parsley	Persil
Pepper	Poivre
Rosemary	Romarin
Tarragon	Estragon
Mixture of herbs	Fines herbes

Potatoes, Rice, and Noodles

Noodles	Nouilles
Pasta	Pâtes
Potatoes	Pommes (de terre)
matchsticks	*allumettes*
mashed and deep-fried	*dauphine*
mashed with butter and egg yolks	*duchesse*
in their jackets	*en robe des champs*
french fries	*frites*
mashed	*mousseline*
boiled/steamed	*nature/vapeur*

Rice	Riz
boiled in bouillon with onions	*pilaf*

Sauces and Preparations

Brown butter, parsley, lemon juice	Meunière
Curry	Indienne
Egg yolks, butter, vinegar	Hollandaise
Hot pepper	Diable
Mayonnaise flavored with mustard and herbs	Tartare
Mushrooms, red wine, shallots, beef marrow	Bordelaise
Onions, tomatoes, garlic	Provençale
Pepper sauce	Poivrade
Red wine, herbs	Bourguignon
Vinegar, egg yolks, white wine, shallots, tarragon	Béarnaise
Vinegar dressing	Vinaigrette
White sauce	Béchamel
White wine, mussel broth, egg yolks	Marinière
Wine, mushrooms, onions, shallots	Chasseur
With goose or duck liver purée and truffles	Périgueux
With Madeira wine	Madère

Cheeses

Mild:	Beaufort
	Beaumont
	Belle étoile
	Boursin
	Brie
	Cantal
	Comté
	Reblochon
	St-Paulin
	Tomme de Savoie
Sharp:	Bleu de Bresse
	Camembert
	Livarot
	Fromage au marc
	Munster
	Pont-l'Évêque
	Roquefort
Swiss:	Emmenthal
	Gruyère
	Vacherin
Goat's milk:	St-Marcellin
	Crottin de Chavignol Valençay
Cheese tart	Tarte au fromage
Small cheese tart	Ramequin
Toasted ham and cheese sandwich	Croque-monsieur

Fruits and Nuts

Almonds	Amandes
Apple	Pomme
Apricot	Abricot
Banana	Banane
Blackberries	Mûres
Blackcurrants	Cassis
Blueberries	Myrtilles
Cherries	Cerises
Chestnuts	Marrons
Coconut	Noix de coco
Dates	Dattes
Dried fruit	Fruits secs
Figs	Figues
Grapefruit	Pamplemousse
Grapes green/blue	Raisin blanc/noir
Hazelnuts	Noisettes
Lemon	Citron
Melon	Melon
Orange	Orange
Peach	Pêche
Peanuts	Cacahouètes
Pear	Poire
Pineapple	Ananas
Plums	Prunes
Prunes	Pruneaux
Raisins	Raisins secs
Raspberries	Framboises
Strawberries	Fraises
Tangerine	Mandarine
Walnuts	Noix
Watermelon	Pastèque

Desserts

Apple pie	Tarte aux pommes
Baked Alaska	Omelette norvégienne
Caramel pudding	Crème caramel
Chocolate cake	Gâteau au chocolat
Chocolate pudding	Mousse au chocolat
Custard tart	Flan
Custard	Creme anglaise
Ice cream	Glace
Layer cake	Tourte
Pear with vanilla ice cream and chocolate sauce	Poire Belle Hélène
Soufflé made with orange liqueur	Soufflé au Grand-Marnier
Sundae	Coupe (glacée)
Water ice	Sorbet
Whipped cream	Crème Chantilly
Creamy dessert of egg yolks, wine, sugar, and flavoring	Sabayon
Puff pastry filled with whipped cream or custard	Profiterole

Index

Personal Itinerary

Departure *Date*

Time

Transportation

Arrival *Date*　　　　*Time*

Departure *Date*　　　　*Time*

Transportation

Accommodations

Arrival *Date*　　　　*Time*

Departure *Date*　　　　*Time*

Transportation

Accommodations

Arrival *Date*　　　　*Time*

Departure *Date*　　　　*Time*

Transportation

Accommodations

Personal Itinerary

Arrival *Date*   *Time*

Departure *Date*   *Time*

Transportation

Accommodations

Arrival *Date*   *Time*

Departure *Date*   *Time*

Transportation

Accommodations

Arrival *Date*   *Time*

Departure *Date*   *Time*

Transportation

Accommodations

Arrival *Date*   *Time*

Departure *Date*   *Time*

Transportation

Accommodations

Personal Itinerary

Arrival	*Date*	*Time*
Departure	*Date*	*Time*
Transportation		
Accommodations		

Arrival	*Date*	*Time*
Departure	*Date*	*Time*
Transportation		
Accommodations		

Arrival	*Date*	*Time*
Departure	*Date*	*Time*
Transportation		
Accommodations		

Arrival	*Date*	*Time*
Departure	*Date*	*Time*
Transportation		
Accommodations		

Personal Itinerary

Arrival *Date*   *Time*

Departure *Date*   *Time*

Transportation

Accommodations

Arrival *Date*   *Time*

Departure *Date*   *Time*

Transportation

Accommodations

Arrival *Date*   *Time*

Departure *Date*   *Time*

Transportation

Accommodations

Arrival *Date*   *Time*

Departure *Date*   *Time*

Transportation

Accommodations

Personal Itinerary

Arrival *Date*   *Time*

Departure *Date*   *Time*

Transportation

Accommodations

Arrival *Date*   *Time*

Departure *Date*   *Time*

Transportation

Accommodations

Arrival *Date*   *Time*

Departure *Date*   *Time*

Transportation

Accommodations

Arrival *Date*   *Time*

Departure *Date*   *Time*

Transportation

Accommodations

Addresses

Name	Name
Address	Address
Telephone	Telephone
Name	Name
Address	Address
Telephone	Telephone
Name	Name
Address	Address
Telephone	Telephone
Name	Name
Address	Address
Telephone	Telephone
Name	Name
Address	Address
Telephone	Telephone
Name	Name
Address	Address
Telephone	Telephone
Name	Name
Address	Address
Telephone	Telephone
Name	Name
Address	Address
Telephone	Telephone

Addresses

Name	*Name*
Address	*Address*
Telephone	*Telephone*
Name	*Name*
Address	*Address*
Telephone	*Telephone*
Name	*Name*
Address	*Address*
Telephone	*Telephone*
Name	*Name*
Address	*Address*
Telephone	*Telephone*
Name	*Name*
Address	*Address*
Telephone	*Telephone*
Name	*Name*
Address	*Address*
Telephone	*Telephone*
Name	*Name*
Address	*Address*
Telephone	*Telephone*

Addresses

Name	Name
Address	Address
Telephone	Telephone
Name	Name
Address	Address
Telephone	Telephone
Name	Name
Address	Address
Telephone	Telephone
Name	Name
Address	Address
Telephone	Telephone
Name	Name
Address	Address
Telephone	Telephone
Name	Name
Address	Address
Telephone	Telephone
Name	Name
Address	Address
Telephone	Telephone
Name	Name
Address	Address
Telephone	Telephone

Fodor's Travel Guides

U.S. Guides

Alaska

Arizona

Boston

California

Cape Cod, Martha's Vineyard, Nantucket

The Carolinas & the Georgia Coast

Chicago

Disney World & the Orlando Area

Florida

Hawaii

Las Vegas, Reno, Tahoe

Los Angeles

Maine, Vermont, New Hampshire

Maui

Miami & the Keys

New England

New Orleans

New York City

Pacific North Coast

Philadelphia & the Pennsylvania Dutch Country

San Diego

San Francisco

Santa Fe, Taos, Albuquerque

Seattle & Vancouver

The South

The U.S. & British Virgin Islands

The Upper Great Lakes Region

USA

Vacations in New York State

Vacations on the Jersey Shore

Virginia & Maryland

Waikiki

Washington, D.C.

Foreign Guides

Acapulco, Ixtapa, Zihuatanejo

Australia & New Zealand

Austria

The Bahamas

Baja & Mexico's Pacific Coast Resorts

Barbados

Berlin

Bermuda

Brazil

Budapest

Budget Europe

Canada

Cancun, Cozumel, Yucatan Penisula

Caribbean

Central America

China

Costa Rica, Belize, Guatemala

Czechoslovakia

Eastern Europe

Egypt

Euro Disney

Europe

Europe's Great Cities

France

Germany

Great Britain

Greece

The Himalayan Countries

Hong Kong

India

Ireland

Israel

Italy

Italy's Great Cities

Japan

Kenya & Tanzania

Korea

London

Madrid & Barcelona

Mexico

Montreal & Quebec City

Morocco

The Netherlands Belgium & Luxembourg

New Zealand

Norway

Nova Scotia, Prince Edward Island & New Brunswick

Paris

Portugal

Rome

Russia & the Baltic Countries

Scandinavia

Scotland

Singapore

South America

Southeast Asia

South Pacific

Spain

Sweden

Switzerland

Thailand

Tokyo

Toronto

Turkey

Vienna & the Danube Valley

Yugoslavia

Special Series

Fodor's Affordables

Affordable Europe

Affordable France

Affordable Germany

Affordable Great
Britain

Affordable Italy

**Fodor's Bed &
Breakfast and
Country Inns Guides**

California

Mid-Atlantic Region

New England

The Pacific Northwest

The South

The West Coast

The Upper Great
Lakes Region

Canada's Great
Country Inns

Cottages, B&Bs and
Country Inns of
England and Wales

The Berkeley Guides

On the Loose in
California

On the Loose in
Eastern Europe

On the Loose in
Mexico

On the Loose in the
Pacific Northwest &
Alaska

**Fodor's Exploring
Guides**

Exploring California

Exploring Florida

Exploring France

Exploring Germany

Exploring Paris

Exploring Rome

Exploring Spain

Exploring Thailand

Fodor's Flashmaps

New York

Washington, D.C.

Fodor's Pocket Guides

Pocket Bahamas

Pocket Jamaica

Pocket London

Pocket New York
City

Pocket Paris

Pocket Puerto Rico

Pocket San Francisco

Pocket Washington,
D.C.

Fodor's Sports

Cycling

Hiking

Running

Sailing

The Insider's Guide
to the Best Canadian
Skiing

**Fodor's Three-In-Ones
(guidebook, language
cassette, and phrase
book)**

France

Germany

Italy

Mexico

Spain

**Fodor's
Special-Interest
Guides**

Cruises and Ports
of Call

Disney World & the
Orlando Area

Euro Disney

Healthy Escapes

London Companion

Skiing in the USA
& Canada

Sunday in New York

**Fodor's Touring
Guides**

Touring Europe

Touring USA:
Eastern Edition

Touring USA:
Western Edition

**Fodor's Vacation
Planners**

Great American
Vacations

National Parks of the
West

**The Wall Street
Journal Guides to
Business Travel**

Europe

International Cities

Pacific Rim

USA & Canada

You'll find the magic
of Provence in these
two acclaimed bestsellers by

Peter Mayle

❧

A YEAR
IN PROVENCE

"Stylish, witty, delightful"
—The Sunday Times, London

"I really loved this book!"
—Julia Child

TOUJOURS
PROVENCE

The New York Times Book Review says:
"It's like returning to a country inn where you
know the owner, where they save your favorite
room for you, and the bartender remembers what
you drink."

*Published in the
United States by*
Alfred A. Knopf, Inc.

*Published in the
United Kingdom by*
Hamish Hamilton, Ltd.